THE BIG Z

THE CARLOS ZAMBRANO STORY

THE BIG Z
THE CARLOS ZAMBRANO STORY

Pedro E. Miranda Torres

TRIUMPH
BOOKS

Triumph Books and colophon are registered trademarks of Random House, Inc.

This book is available in quantity at special discounts for your group or organization. For further information, contact:

Triumph Books
542 South Dearborn Street
Suite 750
Chicago, Illinois 60605
(312) 939-3330 | Fax (312) 663-3557

Printed in U.S.A.
ISBN: 978-1-60078-096-7
Design by Nephtalí Colon of Twelve Tribes Design, and Prologue Publishing Services, LLC. Editorial and page production by Prologue Publishing Services, LLC.

*To the millions of immigrants
who fight for justice in the Diaspora
and do not forget their roots.*

*To Puerto Cabello and its people
for making this story possible.*

*To the city of Chicago
for receiving and loving
the Big Z and his family.*

*To my parents, Elsa and Cucho,
for teaching me the true
value of sports and life.*

*To my children, Emanuel Ernesto,
Andrea Ester, and Daniel Josué,
the reason I live and breathe.*

Blessed are the poor in spirit,
for theirs is the kingdom of heaven.
—The Gospel of Matthew 5:3

Not everything is about money....
I feel comfortable here. I feel good here,
my family feels good here. This is my town,
my home, my city. I love Chicago. I love the Cubs....
Thank God, I can stay here a longer time.
—Carlos Zambrano after signing a
multi-year contract with the Cubs, 2007

CONTENTS

ACKNOWLEDGMENTS

First, I want to thank Tommy Miranda for believing this to be a story worth telling. Also, he believed I could accomplish this task, helped keep me motivated, and provided what was needed in order to help these pages reach the lives of many people in the Caribbean, South America, and the United States. You, along with the Lord who gives life, are the intellectual author of this effort. Your faith that the Big Z's testimony has something to contribute to the world and the magnitude of your compromise give hope to the most pessimistic person. Many thanks. Without you, none of this would have been possible.

Second, I thank Carlos Zambrano, El Toro of Venezuela. The humility and consistent truth of his testimony provide the fundamental framework for this story. His decisive support and collaboration, and his accessibility, make those who know him forget that he is a major league baseball star. We received the same support from all his family, his friends, and the community that saw him grow up from birth to age 16, when he first left his country. To all of you, beloved Puerto Cabello, many thanks for this noble effort. In particular, to Victor, Carlos's brother, who made sure at all times that we had everything we needed for this project. I also want to thank Ismari, the Big Z's wife, for her humility and commitment in helping with this project, and, in particular, for sharing with us their love story. Thanks to Julio Figueroa for being an instrument from God for Carlos and for believing in his possibilities when nobody else did.

Third, I want to thank each and every friend who took the time to read the different drafts. To the Puerto Rican author and editor, Armindo Nuñez Miranda, for a work of excellence; to Dr. Juan "Tito" Meléndez, and to my second cousin, Owen Martínez, for his thoughtful observations and suggestions; to Glorimar Camareno for her collaboration in the translation of the manuscript; to Ana D. Martínez, my coworker in the Puerto Rico Tourism Company for her support in transcribing some of the interviews. I also want to thank Nephtalí Colón and Patricia Soler for the excellent work in graphic design, and photographer Stephen Green for providing some of the photos.

To all of you, to God who renews our hopes, and to all of those whose names are not written down here but have contributed, my deepest expression of gratitude.

INTRODUCTION

Time shows us how God becomes exalted through people in the public eye, especially those involved in the arts and sports. If we take a look at professional baseball, we'll find that some stars have embraced the gospel and have guided others to profess a strong faith in Christ. Because of this, believers use gestures, statements, and testimonies to emphasize how their accomplishments are the result of having God Almighty in their lives.

All the space in the universe is sacred, and sports, like any other human manifestation, is no different—it is firmly under the reach of the divinity. In a world practically absent of sensible and productive leaders, the presence of this young man, born and raised in a place marked by obscurity and hardship, who raised a flag of hope to affirm that there are always possibilities for blessings, success, and abundance, in the best meaning of the word, constitutes a gift from the Creator.

This is about Carlos "the Big Z" Zambrano, one of those luminaries who, from a distant and unexpected place, has demonstrated a powerful faith—a belief so strong he shows the world that it is still possible to trust, even in the midst of material deprivation and emotional or spiritual doubt.

To please the Lord is the main purpose of the Big Z's life. He has been open to receiving the divine mercy for the benefit of the Kingdom which he serves with eagerness and devotion. He has decided not to gloat in his triumphs so that others will know that "the power comes from Jesus Christ." He clearly expressed how his personal and spiritual goals are linked when, on Christmas 2005, he declared, "Next year I am going to win the Cy Young and I am going to place the trophy in the front of my truck with a sign reading: To God Be the Glory!" In the same way, his brother Victor points out that "the Savior knows which one of us He could give success to and he [Carlos] knows who he should give glory for that."

Carlos's success, like that of several baseball players from Venezuela, did not happen in a vacuum. In political terms, Venezuela's relationship with the United States is critical, and at the same time, the country plays an unprecedented leadership role in the contemporary history of the Americas and the world. In the same way, the United States is experiencing a time of great tension concerning Hispanic immigration. With such political unrest, it should not be forgotten that Big Z has been able to become a successful Hispanic in a multi-ethnic nation.

At the same time, the sporting world is also in turmoil, with controversy surrounding the professional ethics of athletes, their physical preparation, and the authenticity of their official statistics. Some big-name, popular players have deceived their fans, their teams, and their sport due to a poor sense of fair competition. This sad reality has forced sports organizations to take drastic and strict measures to protect themselves from the ambition of a few who want to obtain notoriety by means of performance-enhancing drugs.

This lamentable situation has required the intervention of leaders from the professional leagues, members of Congress, and several international organizations, who have investigated the use of anabolic steroids and have adopted rules to penalize its use. The result has been a black mark on professional sports, with both fans and even some players' family members calling into question the validity of recent broken records and Hall of Fame–worthy stats.

The scandal has put professional sports in crisis, which is why the restoration of credibility to enthusiastic fans is such an urgent task. And it's also crucial to draw attention to the testimonies of those baseball players who have worked hard naturally and have turned their backs on immediate but illegal gratification.

For every baseball player who has given in to the seduction of performance-enhancing drugs, there are many more who are proud of their religious faith and practice it openly for the benefit of the sport and their own lives. This is positive not only for the players and the sport—for it may just be what can bring about a revival—but it sets a strong example for the fans. Young people urgently need role models who represent the highest values of faith, justice, excellence, and solidarity.

Zambrano embodies a new vision of reconciliation, motivation, excellence, and hope for our time. His origins, his development as an individual, how he dealt with adversity, and the way in which the triumphs of his life have occurred make this book required reading for those who are searching for a guide to daily excellence, to personal, faith-based success.

El Toro, his nickname in Bolivar's land, is a star pitcher for the Chicago Cubs with an impressive collection of stats: he has been the most stable and consistent pitcher for his team in the past six years; he is the only one to have hit a home run from both sides of the plate—he had six homers in 2006 when he earned his first silver slugger award; he has the fifth-lowest ERA in the major leagues; he batted .300 in 2005; and his fastball is one of the most difficult to hit in the National League. But he is, above all things, a servant of the Good News.

This book describes the origin and upbringing of this disciple of Jesus. We will see his first steps, as, guided by faith, he rose from an impoverished, marginalized area, traveled through the process that led him to sign as a professional ballplayer, worked through professional struggles in the minor leagues, and arrived at Wrigley Field with a successful career in front of him.

Finally, we'll look at the keys that have guided his success and his blessing, learning what he has done to achieve such a strong faith and personal triumph. In the last chapter, the Big Z's professional stats are compiled, and a comparative analysis is presented alongside those of some of the most extraordinary pitchers in the major leagues.

This faith-based look at his life will reveal his victories and challenges, as well as his frustrations. We will observe how Latin baseball players in the United States struggle. Through learning of Carlos's many obstacles, we can find paths to our own personal successes with the sole determination of knowing that with effort and faith "all things are possible." In the same way, we are invited to believe that obstacles in life can call forth our greatest performances and that, after obtaining a goal, we can stand strong in our faith, knowing that we will continue to serve God with enthusiasm and graciousness.

Both believers and non-believers, athletes and couch potatoes, baseball fanatics and non-sports enthusiasts, those with reserved character and those with gregarious spirit, Latinos and people from other ethnic backgrounds, all alike will find an extraordinary example of what it is to gain fame and fortune but still remain humble and maintain the highest aspiration of trying to live for the glory of God.

THE BIG Z

THE CARLOS ZAMBRANO STORY

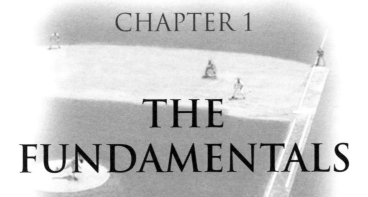

CHAPTER 1

THE
FUNDAMENTALS

But God chose the foolish of the world to shame the wise.
—I Corinthians 1:27

The life of Carlos Zambrano is that of the eagle that flies in the middle of a storm and, facing opposing winds, ascends powerfully until it reaches the top of the mountains.

No one in his family ever thought that the unstable, aggressive, and spirited young man, filled with brute force and nicknamed, appropriately, "El Toro" (Spanish for "bull"), would transform as time passed into a recognized and respected athlete. As even he admits, he was "very clumsy in sports" and not very dedicated in academic affairs.

Carlos comes from the Cumboto II neighborhood, part of the urban area of Puerto Cabello, a city in the state of Carabobo, Venezuela. This is a small community of poor but happy people, hard workers, located only minutes from the most important harbor in Venezuela. There is another Cumboto, Cumboto I, where people with better economic resources live, but that's a very different place—similar to Carlos's hometown in name alone.

The Zambrano family arrived in Cumboto II after being displaced from La Isla, an area where they had lived for several years and where, later on, a portion of the harbor mentioned above was built. According to Saulo Zambrano, Carlos's

The view of Puerto Cabello from the Big Z's apartment balcony, November 2005.

The Zambrano family was moved from sector La Isla to Cumboto II, due to the construction of the port in the early 1980s. Their home, second from the right, now rebuilt and two stories, is not even a shadow of the humble home full of strong values where the Zambranos were raised. At the end there is the Tower, the community playground.

Nora's sister Aunt Edesia's house. From this kitchen and this home came food in times of need for the Zambrano family, January 2006.

father, "The times in La Isla were of much scarcity. We lived in sort of a ranch where we had problems with the water. Due to this situation, the government decided to move the community and allowed us to live in an area in Cumboto II."

It has been said that Puerto Cabello received its name because the Spanish, at the time of the conquest, upon seeing the tranquil waters of the coastal shore, said that in those waters you could anchor a ship to the pier with a single hair.

In the midst of this tropical paradise, a tranquil and peaceful ocean, a developing city on the rise, but in a neighborhood filled with misery and misfortune, El Toro was born. He grew up as one of God's children, under the protection of his parents, Nora and Saulo, and along with six brothers, Johnny, Dennis, Victor, Derwin, Yormis, and Ermys.

In his formative years, Carlos wasn't viewed by those around him as someone who would grow up to be a sports superstar. When he finally did became a member of a baseball team—through his determination and tenacity alone—

his potential on the ball diamond went unnoticed. He was the kid who only came off of the bench during the last innings just to make sure everyone had participated in the game. His family and friends remember that he always invited them to come watch him play whenever he had games, but he was never called to the field and would spend the whole game sitting on the bench. His coaches said that he didn't have the appropriate mechanics and that he pitched recklessly. Nonetheless, everyone admitted that he was very strong.

Over time, Carlos continued to practice and to study the game of baseball and the art of pitching. His skills improved, his pitching became more accurate, and, thanks to the support of his family and his first mentor, Julio Figueroa, he became good enough to try out for the majors. But when he went to his first tryout, he was not considered a prime player. Representatives from the major league teams were indeed interested—and they did sign him—but he wasn't offered the top dollar amounts other players were being offered. His first few years in the league, the Big Z didn't receive the money he deserved. In fact, before signing his new contract in the summer of 2007, his salary compared to other pitchers with a comparable number of years in the league was much lower, despite having much better stats. His true value was finally recognized in 2007 when he did sign a new five-year contract and also became a strong contender for the prestigious Cy Young Award.

His first team was called Carisma, and his first coach was José Guadalupe Alvarado. Alvarado remembered Carlos from his early years. He said:

He was a pre-teen then. I remember asking him if he wanted to play baseball, and he said soccer; but I talked to his parents several times, and they finally gave him permission. When I threw about 50 balls at him and he did not even hit so much as a foul, I realized that he did not have natural skill. In that moment, I told him that I was going to try him as a pitcher because I truly thought he was going to be a pitcher. When he pitched, I could tell even then he had a strong fast-ball....Seeing him in the major leagues is marvelous.

CHAPTER 2

LIFE SYNOPSIS OF THE BIG Z

And we know that in all things God works for the good…
of those who love him, who have been called
according to his purpose.
—Romans 8:28

The origin of Carlos Zambrano-Matos, better known as El Toro or the Big Z in the city of Chicago, goes back two decades to the displacement from La Isla to Puerto Cabello, the place where one of the most important harbors in Venezuela is today. At that time, the government allowed the Zambrano-Matos family a small parcel of land with a small wooden house, where the parents and their seven children shared a mere three bedrooms.

Carlos's mother, Nora, recalls that there were days when they did not have a cent for food and the boys cried because they had nothing to eat. In such moments, which were not few, her sister Edesia Matos brought them food when she could. Her husband was a street vendor, and he and Edesia were always willing to share whatever they could with the young family. Maybe that is why the Big Z knows for a fact that, as he puts it, God "squeezes hard but does not choke you."

However, not everything was about scarcity. Carlos did have a good childhood. His favorite activities included soccer, baseball—with a ball made out of a sock—and, later on, video games, which he still plays and enjoys like a kid. The ballpark was rough, with an uneven field and a tower that served as an unsightly landmark for the town of Cumboto II.

It was hardscrabble land, filled with rocks and weeds, but it also was a place of fun, tradition, and neighborhood culture.

Nevertheless, the Big Z had big dreams. From an early age, growing up in a neighborhood otherwise forgotten by progress and prestige and without ever having been part of a baseball team, young Carlos looked out over the uneven field, the ugly tower, the weeds, and the sky, and, with faith in God, dreamt that he would some day make it big. While

La Torre, or the Tower, the community playground in Cumboto II, was Carlos's first ball field.

The school that serves the Cumboto II neighborhood.

he used a broomstick and a sock ball, he dreamt that one day he would be swinging a Louisville Slugger at a ball with the Major League Baseball logo on it. He believed it without knowing it, without seeing it.

Carlos Alberto—the two names mean nobility and strength—received Christian teachings, like all his brothers, at home and at Sunday school in his church in Puerto Cabello, Iglesia Evangélica Pentecostal Monte Horeb, under the leadership of the Reverend Manuel Colmenares. Every family member attended church regularly every Sunday and on special days, where they received the spiritual foundation that still guides the family today. The church was and still is an extremely important part of the Zambrano family's life— most of them still are a part of that same faith community.

As a child, Carlos was always interested in sports but, due to his family's poverty, he could not afford to join an organized team. His life then revolved around the neighborhood, the church, and the ballfield.

When he was a teenager, Carlos experienced something that would change his life forever. He joined Carisma, his first baseball team. The word *carisma* has a very important significance since its root meaning in Greek is "grace," which implies happiness and is a gift from God. Carlos believed that he had been given the skills to play baseball from God. Through this special talent, he believed he could spread a message of hope, even when no one saw in him even a hint of his true capabilities, even when his family had no money to sign him up to play on a team.

Talent, Carlos believes, is not necessarily tied to the quality of one's personality or the natural abilities with which a person is born. A talent is a gift from God to be used for a specific end, meaning spiritual enlightenment. He stayed dedicated because he believed he had been given the talent in order to change others' lives for the better. For that reason, a friend of the family and former classmate, nicknamed El Orejón (which means "the one with big ears"), remembered that the Big Z's friends abandoned the dedication for the sport, but he never did. "What he accomplished was because of his effort and dedication. He never gave up and he moved forward. Let's not talk about talent...no. He wanted it and he did it. And I feel a part of that achievement," said El Orejón.

After his first experience as a children's league player in his neighborhood, the Big Z continued to develop in the youth leagues in Puerto Cabello. As he grew older, he progressed through the leagues, first in the junior league, then in pre-juvenile, and later in the juvenile league, although only for a short time. He never stood out enough to be seen as a possible draftee for the major leagues until he had the opportunity to pitch against a major league–quality prospect in a game in the juvenile league. Towards the end of the game, he was put in to pitch to the best hitter on the opposing team. The Big Z's brother, Dennis, was watching from the bleachers, along with a recruiter and pitching coach named Julio Figueroa. Julio, in fact, was there to scout the hitter, who was a major league prospect. Carlos arrived to the mound and, after hearing the usual criticism he was already used to, he threw four pitches to dramatically strike out the player who had been, until then, the center of attention.

At that precise moment, Julio, who had known Carlos since childhood, realized that the Big Z had the potential to develop as a professional baseball player. As Julio has himself admitted, when Carlos first was invited to start training, he was not fully aware of his potential. Julio wanted to help, but he couldn't exactly tell how much this young guy could do. On top of that, when he did begin working with Carlos, Julio was criticized by others in the community for wasting so much time on someone who didn't show enough talent. Their negative comments backfired, though, because it had just the opposite effect, inspiring Julio to prove them all wrong. It gave them both the strength to continue Carlos's development as an athlete.

Julio Figueroa became the Big Z's volunteer trainer and coach. They ran and trained several times a week. And, even though Julio did not know Carlos's full potential at the start, he devoted himself fully to the training of the young ballplayer. Julio had faith—the faith that maybe some near him did not have. He helped get rid of the dross and polish the gold in the Big Z.

In his training, both Carlos and his trainer jogged a two-kilometer steep route up the hill that started at the entrance to Cumboto II, passing through Mercado Libre, and on up to the Solano Fort in the San Esteban National Park. When they reached the top, they worked on his pitching mechanics, and Julio would constantly remind Carlos about the importance of maintaining such a crucial workout.

As his training progressed and he started to show noticeable improvement, his interest in church activities began to wane. He himself has said that, at the time, he had lost the desire to attend church. Like many teenagers, he turned away from the community of faith in which he had grown up.

During that same time, his parents began a process of visiting several other churches. And though he no longer had a strong interest in religion, Carlos didn't abandon his church home altogether. He recalls that "even though we were visiting other churches, my heart never moved away from Monte Horeb, and in some way I always visited the church. There was a moment when I became independent and I started going to church by myself, even though there were only about eight to 10 members and it was about to close down." When speaking about this experience, he concludes by admitting that "deep down I felt that my life would only be complete by being with the Lord."

The congregation at Monte Horeb and their pastor Manuel Colmenares knew how to face such challenges. At that time, a movement arose within the church named Royal Rangers. The Royal Rangers movement is devoted to reaching out to children and teenagers in Christ's name. It was created by the Assemblies of God Church in 1962, and has expanded as much in Latin America as it has in the U.S. In Venezuela, there are now more than 250,000 Royal Rangers, and its numbers continue to grow.

A chapter at Monte Horeb was founded to help motivate the young people who attended church to get involved in this initiative. "Commander Freddie," a youth leader who later became the Big Z's assistant, has stated that the Royal Rangers helped Carlos stay close to church life. The kids involved in Royal Rangers, as with those in many youth groups, had to raise money for trips and events. Among the fund-raising activities they held were selling guava bread

Fortin Solano, where the Big Z had his first trainings with Julio Figueroa and developed his pitching skills.

and garbage bags. People from the neighborhood and church community remember that the Big Z would sell some of the bread, but would eat some as well, and his female cousins on his mother's side would pay for his travel expenses because they saw how hard he was trying. Freddie also remembers that Carlos's youth leader would always pair him with Ismari, even though they did not get along. In one of the

Pastor Manuel Colmenares gets inside the van that the Big Z gave him as a birthday present. He's been the Zambrano family's spiritual leader for more than 20 years, December 2005.

Royal Rangers retreats, Carlos and Ismari got to know each other more and eventually fell in love.

Through the Royal Rangers, Monte Horeb was capable of widening the concept of spirituality in order to attract teenagers to the church. Such creativity is what allows the church to stay relevant in the lives of Christian youth and to maintain a solid and faithful congregation.

In this process, one can see how the Big Z was able to gain strength in the midst of adversity. He remembers one of his first youth leaders, Magali Ortiz. On the day of her wedding, the Rangers were to be the court of honor, standing in uniform. The Big Z did not have the money to pay for a uniform, but, even without one, he bravely stood up at the wedding. That day, he walked with the strength of a chosen one who knows that his dignity does not depend on external things but on the will of not giving up or feeling shame when faced with difficult times.

The Big Z, even with his baseball celebrity, continues to this day as a youth pastor, working with young people in his native Venezuela. Some of the things that he has designed with his staff are baseball and softball games to attract young people. Conquer the City, his pastoral team, is formed precisely by those who grew up with him as part of the Royal Rangers.

The process of achieving his lifelong goal to become a professional baseball player was plagued by difficulties, rejection, and missed opportunities. The first team to see him was the Cubs, who of course later signed him in Chicago, but before this, three other teams saw him play in Venezuela and had their chance.

The first experience with the Cubs, whose personnel had just arrived in Puerto Cabello, did not lead to positive results. The most important of their scouts did not even see him then, though he sent one of his underlings to watch the Big Z play. Later, he was noticed and scouted by the Toronto Blue Jays, the Florida Marlins, the Arizona Diamondbacks, and again, and for the last time, the Cubs.

The rest, as they say, is history. The Big Z has proven himself to be among the best baseball players in the world. He is also the youth pastor of the Iglesia Evangélica Pentecostal Monte Horeb in Puerto Cabello, Venezuela, and owns a computer business, the Cyber Bull Cafe, that employs close to 20 people. The majority of these employees are relatives or people who grew up with him. In the meantime, he has helped many people in his community, both known and unknown, affirming his social responsibility with the people who are a part of his triumphs, who helped make him who he is.

CHAPTER 3

ORIGINS
AS TOLD BY THE BIG Z

That boy is surly, he is brave, like a bull.
—Beatriz, maternal aunt, when nicknaming Carlos

Christ sets me free.
—Carmen Matos, maternal grandmother

El Toro's apartment was full of relatives, including three of his brothers with their wives and children. It was a battalion divided in the traditional way: women in the kitchen and men in the living room watching sports or playing PlayStation. The idea of conducting an interview with so many people around was kind of worrying. Nevertheless, after a succulent breakfast of Venezuelan-style *arepas*, we went into the bedroom in order to have some privacy. This was a sign of his openness, which altered my hypothesis that communication between us would be difficult since baseball players, in general, are people of very few words.

Ismari, his wife, and Tommy Miranda, his friend and agent, were with us during the interview. I sat on a stool, the couple on the bed, and Tommy in a chair next to me. With jokes and stories—the usual way among the Zambranos—I started the conversation.

Pedro Miranda: I want to share with you a Bible text that can be a good start for our conversation. When I began learning about your life, these were the verses that came to my mind: "Because the foolishness of God is wiser than men, and the weakness of God is stronger than men.

"For you see your calling, brethren, that not many wise according to the flesh, not many mighty, not many noble, are called. But God has chosen the foolish things of the world to put to shame the wise, and God has chosen the weak things of the world to put to shame the things which are mighty; and the base things of the world and the things which are despised. God has chosen the things which are not, to bring to nothing the things that are, that no flesh should glory in His presence." (1 Corinthians 1:25-29)

Big Z: Really! *He answered excitedly.* I was reading those verses and I was going to go get my Bible to start with that text, in the name of God...

Why?

Because I believe in what God has done in my life and in the life of many foolish people, scorned people, people who were considered the worst of the world, but He has given them His grace. He lifts them up from where they are, and now they are ministers, people who God wants for His ministry. Understand?

How were those first years, the process of growing up, of building the foundation of who Carlos Zambrano is today?

Even when we were little, we were a humble family. We grew up, basically, in poverty since we did not have many resources. My father was a hard worker and he raised us to be that way. He taught us to earn our daily bread with our sweat, to conduct ourselves properly in life, and to be honest. We were not raised with bad habits. There are seven brothers in the family, and we always had cousins around us. I remember that we always went to summer league, and since I was the youngest, I was not allowed to play because you had to be 15 to play and I was just five or six; but I would go with my brothers and I enjoyed seeing them play ball.

(above) Half of Big Z's brothers in his condo terrace in Puerto Cabello. From left: el Gordo, Pedro (author), Big Z, Vitico, and el Niño, September 2005.

(right) Johnny and Dennys, Big Z's older twin brothers.

(below) Nora and Ermis "el Negro," the youngest of the Big Z's brothers.

(I remember his mother Nora and her comments about those first years, which I gathered in a later dialogue.

Nora Zambrano: Those were difficult times to raise seven boys with needs and difficulties. After the twins [Johnny and Dennis] were born, we arrived in Cumboto II. It was not easy to find a job, so they suffered a great deal. I was always a home-maker and their father was a truck driver. Then, when the fifth boy was born, he started working with the fiber for furniture and anything else that would come up. Sometimes he was with-out a job for up to four months. After the twins turned 16, since they did not want to keep studying, they went to work. In spite of everything, God has blessed us...maybe because He saw that there was unity between us and that we were not avaricious people. Even with all the difficulties and needs, I never left them to go to work and have luxury. I kept struggling with our needs and, whenever we got some money, I would buy something. But like the Bible says, "My thoughts are not your thoughts." It is hard when you have so many debts and still your young chil-dren are crying of hunger. Sometimes at noon we still did not have anything to eat. The oldest children did not cry but had sad looks on their faces. It is hard. They cried because they were hungry. But all those struggles are gone, and I thank God for that and what He has done through Carlos.)

Carlos, how did your passion for baseball start?

I believe it's been there since I was a young child, when my younger brother went to the leagues and my father would take me along. To continue the story, we were seven brothers and we lived in a small, three-bedroom house. Two of the bedrooms were for all seven boys and one was for my parents. I remember that my brother Victor [the third child] and I slept on a full-sized bed and another brother slept on a hammock placed over us, so if he fell, he would fall right over us in the middle of the night. But the hammock was well reinforced, thanks to my father's expertise. Another brother slept in the other room, while others slept in the living room. We were poor but had a good life. We did suffer hunger. On occasions, there was nothing to eat in the afternoon, and our stomachs had not yet even a bite to eat. I remember that my grandma, Carmen Matos, along with my aunt Edesia, would come over at around 3:00 PM with a bag of flour. I remember them both as the two people who were always watching over us and always bringing us something. God never let us go to bed with empty stomachs.

You can say that since you were a little child, you have experienced God's provision.

Definitely, yes. There is an old saying that "God squeezes but does not choke you," and many times we were tight. I do not believe that He squeezes, but one squeezes him or herself. God allows us to go through many trials that serve as experiences, but I am sure He does not choke you, for He is always willing to listen to the prayers of the servant and He is always ready to fill you up. Sometimes you have to walk part of the path so God can fulfill His plan. He tells you when is enough because He has provided in a special way and has manifested Himself in a successful way. I believe that we had a happy childhood even though we were poor. It was a very happy childhood at age five, six, and seven. My father was a very strict person and careful when it was time to give us permission to go out. I believe that helped us be better citizens and unbind ourselves from the things that did not please God. Our father would tell us, "You will go from this corner to that corner, and you will not go farther from there or you will have a problem with me." Maybe sometimes we moved a bit farther, but we always followed every letter of what he said. If our father said that we had to be home by a certain time, we had to be

The Big Z is very fierce and intense during his games, and he's not shy about showing it.

home at that time, for he was a very strict person, and we were afraid that he would scold us or spank us or something else that we didn't want.

(I share with you a story told by his brother Victor when we met in Puerto Rico for the Baseball Classics in 2006. He said that his father was so strict that one time all the children got together and made him a sign on his bedroom door that read: "The Captain." When his father saw it, he got very angry, but Victor remembered the story with laughter.)

Was your father affectionate?

Yes, even though he was strict, he was very affectionate. He would carry us when we were little, and he still does. My father is a person who, in spite of his character and his temper, still asks us, "Tell me, how are you doing?" Whenever I go home to Venezuela after the season, and he has not had a chance to travel to see me in Chicago and hasn't seen me for eight months or so, and I see him for the first time, he will cry and say, "Look at my young man. It is so good to have you here." And he will let the tears out.

I was watching you pitch in the game this past weekend, and I remember seeing you on television on another occasion, and I can tell that you are very fierce and intense in your game. You slam your glove if something goes wrong, talk to yourself; you are very expressive. Where do you get that eagerness and energy from?

First of all, it is part of my character. I believe that each one of us has a little bit of the Zambrano in us, as we say. That is transmitted in the intensity when I pitch. When I was a little boy and I would see other children play, and when they made a mistake, they were kind of apathetic, and I would say to myself, "That guy does not have the blood for baseball." I cannot make a mistake and not do anything because I like to do things right, almost perfectly, particularly when playing baseball. I have to play with intensity and put love into what I am doing. Like when I used to play soccer.

(On the cover of the December 2005 issue of Vine Line *magazine, the official magazine of the Chicago Cubs, the Big Z appears wearing a baseball glove in his left hand and a soccer ball in the right hand.)*

I have always played with love and passion. It is true that sometimes my nerves betray me. I am a very nervous person, and sometimes I start shaking my hands or moving the glove or making certain gestures. Sometimes I calm down because I know that it is just what happens in the game.

Why are you called El Toro?

Look, of all my brothers, I believe I am the surly one. I am the kind of person who would react quickly to some things, but although not easy to see, I am quiet, and you can ask my wife about that.

We'll ask her later.

(Laughs) I am very calm, but when I get mad, I act like a Zambrano. That's the bad part, although I think I have made

some progress. When I was little, like 10 months or a year old and I was learning to walk, when people tried to reach for me because I was chubby, I could not let them help me. One day, my maternal aunt, Beatriz Matos, agitated by this behavior, exclaimed, "That boy is surly, he is brave, like a bull." From then on, people started calling me El Toro. The nickname has nothing to do with baseball, but with my personality since my childhood.

(Now I turn to Ismari, who has returned from tending to the youngest of the girls.)

Ismari, how did you two meet?

Ismari Zambrano: I arrived at the church in Puerto Cabello when I was 14 or 15 years old, and that is when we first met. There was a league called Royal Rangers, something like the Boy Scouts today but church-oriented. We were part of that group, nevertheless, everything was not peachy. In the beginning we did not get along.

(El Toro cannot control his need to react, and so he does.)

Big Z: She hated me.

IZ: Yes, I did not like him because he was a repellent. Repellent was used to kill bugs, and that's what we called the people we didn't like. I used to call him that because he couldn't see me without bothering me, and we bashed heads. I would tell him, "What did I do to you that you have to bother me so much?"

(El Toro interrupts again.)

Big Z: Yes, I teased her and made jokes, but it wasn't because I didn't like her. I would see her and say things like, "There is that chubby girl coming this way." Anything. But people would make jokes and bug me, even the leader of the brigade [Freddie] made fun about it, and I would respond, "Don't joke about me and that girl because she is very ugly." From all of that, love started to grow. Well, she can tell you.

(Ismari talks again.)

IZ: Later I started seeing the human side of him, and I realized he was very affectionate, very attentive, and very playful. I always knew he was playful because he was the one to start the parties at church. One day we went to a Youth Congress of the Assemblies of God Churches that usually took place in the beginning of the year in Venezuela, and there I realized I was in love with him because other girls were joking about it. I got so mad that I had to ask myself, "Why does this bother me?"

(In that moment her eyes sparkle, and El Toro makes playful gestures, showing he is pleased with what his love is saying.)

By the time of that event, we had been getting to know each for a year or two.

So your relationship was solely based on teasing each other up to that moment?

Yes, that was the greatest moment. It was very cold up there and I was not dressed appropriately for the cold. We had planned to go see a tourist destination and I had nothing to wear. He took off his sweater so I could wear it to go on the outing, and he told me that he didn't mind being cold but that I deserved to go on the outing and see everything there was to see there. The rest is history.

Who asked whom?

Well, we were in the group, and sometimes we had our encounters and troubles. The youth leader always paired us up when we had to go sell fund-raising items.

(I interrupt to tell the story that Ismari's father, Ismael Borges, told me about the first time the Big Z went to his house to sell garbage bags without knowing that Ismari lived there. He greeted her father and then saw Ismari. He was surprised to see that she lived there. From then on, he always went to the

house. When it was time to ask for her hand in marriage, her father remembers that the Big Z was very nervous even though her father already knew what Carlos was going to ask. The Big Z couldn't say a word until he admitted that he was Ismari's boyfriend.)

Selling fund-raising items was part of the work plan to earn money to pay the Youth Congress. The youth leader always assigned us in the same group. I did not want to be in the same group and complained.

But you really didn't mean it?

I was very emphatic about it, "Noooo!"

Big Z: In that moment we were still at odds because she was not in love with me yet. When the Congress happened, she took notice of me, and I started to like her. After the event, we started looking at each other in a different way, "with a sparkle in our eyes." We would see each other in church, but I wouldn't say a word because I was very, very shy, and we kept selling the garbage bags and bread on the streets. The brigade was formed by a group of 40 young people between 13 and 15 years old. After that, we started working on the Royal Rangers youth camp to be held in February. Then I remember that one day, when the jokes had amounted to so much, we started falling in love. I approached a guy who used to sit with her at church and I told him, "Go tell Ismari something for me, love stuff." Instead of telling her what I had told him, he would tell her other things that she did not understand.

What things?

IZ: He [Carlos] would tell him to tell me that he was in love with me and ask if he had any hope. But when the guy came to me, he would tell me that Carlos was after me but that "he is not worth it because here I am." That is what he would say. "Stop growing illusions about Carlos."

*The Big Z and his wife,
Ismari, shared secret
looks and made each
other laugh throughout
their interview in their
Chicago condo.*

The name, the name...

IZ: *(Laughs)*

(Big Z answers.)

Big Z: No, no, I cannot say, but his name is Franklin.

IZ: *(Laughs)* He knows the story and, if he reads it some day, he will laugh like we are laughing now.

(They tell that Franklin is very close to the family and he is an active supporter of the Big Z's ministry.)

Big Z: Well, the thing is that he always did that. When I went on a trip with my oldest brother and would leave messages for her, it seems like he never gave her the messages.

We then went to the camp and it was like a jungle, a place very far from the city where we camped for five days.

(Ismari interrupts.)

IZ: No, the camp lasted seven days.

Big Z: The first night I was watching to see if she would go out of the camp with her girlfriends, but she was not there, and I thought, "Could she be with a guy from another camp? Could it be that someone else is after her?"

(At this point, Carlos and Ismari exchange several looks at one another.) What about those looks?

"Deep loving looks." *(Laughs)*

On the bus from Puerto Cabello to Espíritu, where the camp was, I approached a guy named Yandi and I sent her messages. He sat with Ismari, and I sat in the chair in front of them. I wanted to ask him to let me sit in his seat, but I was shy. Afterwards, I would send her messages which he would deliver in full. I once told Yandi that I wanted to talk to her about my love for her, but since her mother was there and she was very strict, I had to be discreet. I asked him to tell her to wait for me at a certain place. We finally got together and I remember there was a full moon.

(Ismari continues.)

IZ: There was a campfire that night. A big campfire. Around it, they did a little play.

Big Z: We got together with David, Yandi, and the other guy through whom I sent messages to her sometimes. We were talking, when all of them said, "We will be back." Little by little, they all left us alone. But since I was so shy, as I told you, I sat there and thought, "Now what do I do?" I did not say a word for about five minutes. Ask her.

IZ: I think he waited longer.

Big Z: I was stuttering, and she was waiting to hear what I had to say. I finally said, "You know that I like you."

(Laughs) We started talking and we kissed on the cheek and we left there as boyfriend and girlfriend. Six months later we kissed on the lips for the first time.

Six months! Why?

Because I was really shy and so was she. We always saw each other at her house and we were not going to kiss at her house and act as a couple since I had not talked to her father yet.

IZ: Nor at church because neither my parents nor the people from church knew.

Big Z: Her parents did not know, and I had not told the pastors, get it? I visited her house, but not as her boyfriend, as a visitor. I always took a friend with me.

IZ: The excuse was that my father made this concentrated pineapple juice that tasted like wine, and every time they came over, they would tell my father, "We want wine."

Big Z: We wanted wine and came over to spend some time with you. But it was a lie, my interest had a name and it was Ismari because we were already dating and that was the way we could see each other. We talked but we did not kiss or anything. It was the same at church. You know where we first kissed?

Where?

At Pastor's Colmenares house. There were only two girls there, Rosalinda and Yoquina, and suddenly we realized they were gone.

(Quickly, they clarify…)

No, they didn't leave. They were on the couch in the living room. We were in the kitchen.

IZ: Yes, in the kitchen. We looked at each other, and looked at each other again. Then we kissed on the lips for the first time.

Who took the first step? (Big Z rushes a blunt answer.)
Big Z: Me
Can you give me more details?
It was not so long, like 20 minutes. *(Laughs)* By that time
I was already training in Chicago. Chicago was bringing me
to the United States, and that is when I talked to her parents.
Is that the time when you were signed as a baseball player?
I was in that process.
*I understand that you didn't play baseball when you were
little, that it wasn't until you were a teenager when you joined
your first team. At what age did you really get started playing
baseball?*
I always played soccer and baseball in the streets and in
the landfill in Cumboto II with my brothers and friends. In
an organized way, I started at age 13 because my parents
would tell me every year that they were going to sign me up,
but they didn't have money for that. My little brother was
the one that the owner of the team always looked for. He was
her favorite. So I played on the streets.
*(The house where Big Z grew up was located on a dirt
road and, at the end, there was a land that is now abandoned.
That was their playing field. It's located near a canal, and
there is an electricity tower, which is why it's called "La
Torre" (the tower). Every afternoon, the neighborhood kids
would go out and play with paper or sock balls tied up with
tape and using pieces of wood as bats to play baseball and
feed their dreams. Derwin, one of his brothers, remembers
that on one occasion the bats were broken, and the Big Z,
kneeling down, said that he was going to hit a home run for
him. He knelt down, took the wood bat, and knocked it out of
the park—or at least the land that was their stadium.
Dickson, his childhood friend, tells that while they played,
when he saw an airplane, the Big Z would say, "You'll see*

that some day I am going to ride in an airplane to play base-
ball in the United States.")

How did you feel when you were not signed up year after
year?

I always said that I wanted to play organized baseball. I
wanted to know what that was like. Since the time I was little, I was a bad baseball player. That is why the Bible text
that you read in the beginning is perfect for me, because I
was horrible at baseball. I did not catch well. I was okay at
the bat, but I had a good arm. God developed that arm, and
that is how I got signed. I always played on the streets. I was
the first one there. I was a big fan of baseball and soccer.

Which sport is your passion? You also mentioned soccer. You
always liked to be in the game field, but due to money limita-
tions you where never part of an organized team.

In order to play, you had to register and pay some money
for the registration. That money was used for uniforms, paying the umpires, the team expenses during the game season.
Teams sometimes did not have all the money.

Not everyone could pay.

Not everyone could pay, but my brother didn't have to pay
because the owner of the team wanted him on the team so
badly that she didn't charge him. I kept playing around with
my friends. When I was 13, I don't know how it happened,
but I registered for the team. I really don't remember how,
but I started playing. I played right field and sometimes I
pitched.

How was that first experience?

It was pretty good, considering I had never seen the
umpire or faced a real pitcher in that category. It was a very
exciting experience. The next year I played in the junior
league, and there was always a group who would move on
together to the next category. I remember one time when I

went in to sign up, when I was 13, and I told the owner, "I want to sign up for your team." She replied, "And where do you think you are going to play?" I could play anywhere, I told her, and then she said, "Do you think you can play better than them?" She was very discouraging to me, but I kept trying my hardest, at this level and all the other levels I passed through.

Did you ever feel like going back home?

No, no, because I had the desire to play organized baseball. When I got to junior, we had a very good season, and in the second year I was on Team B because in Venezuela, when the teams had many members, they divide them in A and B. Team A is the stronger one, where the good players are placed—those who are good at batting—and Team B has the not-so-good ones, the more-or-less average players. The owner once said, "I am going to have to get rid of Team B because they are affecting Team A." When we heard about that, we confronted her and we told her that she could not do that just because she thought we were garbage. The coach didn't like that either, and he also confronted her. At the end, we won and were qualified, even though Team B did not usually qualify. We were then eliminated on the first round of the playoffs.

Were you already pitching then?

Yes, I was pitching.

(I remember something Carlos's father had told me earlier about his attitude toward sports in raising his seven sons. He felt he had made a mistake in discouraging them from playing sports, telling them it was more important to him that they stayed in church instead of on the field. "They always played secretly, and of course I always knew," he said. "Now I think in a different way. You can please God doing sports.")

When did you have the chance of becoming a pitcher?

Julio Figueroa met the Big Z when he was pitching in the juvenile leagues. He trained with Carlos, teaching him the importance of pitching fundamentals, and set up the tryout with the Cubs.

We were in the juvenile category, and there was a guy named Luis Aguillones. He was a person of many talents back then, and I thought he was going to be signed and go very far. While we were playing a round robin series, I had to pitch against him. I struck him out. Julio Figueroa, one of the most important persons in my life and my career, was in the audience. I had known him all my life, since he played with my brother Dennis in Venezuela. My brother had said to him, "I have a brother who bats like Andrés Galarraga." Julio was in the audience and so was my brother. When we were losing the game, they let me pitch since I was always assigned at the end. I pitched against the best batter, the prospect, and I struck him out with four fastballs. Surprised, Julio asked my brother, "Is that your brother?" My brother answered that I was the one who resembled Galarraga.

At the end of the game, people used to stick around to have a beer and hang out. That day, my brother stayed longer and, since I was catching a ride with him, I had to stick around while he and Julio hung out. Julio then started talking to me and he told my brother, "You know, I have a friend who is part of the organization in Toronto named Pedro Ávila. If you want, we can train to find out what they have to say." He then told me, "Look, Carlos, do you want to start training to see if I can hook you up with Pedro Ávila?" I then answered, "Sure, of course." That is when I started training.

I started running, and I remember that I had these leather shoes with a thick sole that I wore when running. Julio trained with me twice a week in the beginning because he was working. When he retired, he dedicated himself to training me. We went everywhere asking for rides. One day he left the stadium angry and told me, "Carlos, I don't have money for the bus." I then told him, "Julio, I'm hungry," and he said, "Me, too, let's go get something to drink." We were going for this thick drink made out of rice. He said, "Let's go, but if we have a drink, we won't have money and we'll have to walk or ask for a ride." We bought the drink and we stood outside the stadium to ask for a ride. Then my father came by in an old Volkswagen, a car from the 1960s. He asked us what had happened, and we said that we were just asking for a ride. He gave us a ride. He was fixing that car that belonged to a cousin named Natanael, and Julio said, "See, Carlos, we found a ride and didn't go hungry." That is one of the many things that happened.

I practiced pitching with him, and Julio started teaching me the basics of pitching since I was very raw. I would lean backwards too much and would open myself up too much during the movement. I didn't know how to do any of these things. I didn't know how to pitch, which is fundamental. I remember Julio telling me, "Carlos, it's not like that; this is the way." I would do it wrong, would pitch high, and I didn't want to pitch high because I wanted to pitch in the strike zone. I would tell myself, "This isn't going to work because these exercises are too hard." But we kept practicing and practicing until I finally, sort of, got it, and Julio worked very hard with me on that. There were moments when he would pick me up in the morning and again in the afternoon to train.

Did he believe in you?

Yes. We were out all the time, and people would tell him, "What are you doing with that guy? You'll be signed before he is." He never told me what people were saying. He kept training me while people shouted that I had no future, that I was too skinny, that I didn't pitch hard enough. In spite of people's comments, he was very firm. In the afternoons, after we trained, we would go to his house and he would fix me this meal made out of cereal, bananas, milk, and oatmeal cookies to help me gain weight. His house was not too far from mine. I had to cross a highway. We would talk in his house, and he would always give me advice. Sometimes we would go see a major league game on TV at a friend's house. He would tell me to learn the baseball pitches and how the players were batting.

When did you sign?

The first tryout that I went to was organized by the Chicago Cubs. They were the first and the last team to see me. We were training one day when Julio told me, "I have good news. The people from Chicago have an academy in a place called Vejuma, near Topolito, in the state of Valencia." They were thinking about moving the academy to Puerto Cabello, so they were training in Valencia, even though they were also training twice a week in Puerto Cabello. After that January, they completely moved to Puerto Cabello. Julio told me, "I have arranged a tryout for February 27."

What year are we talking about?

Chicago Cubs' Puerto Cabello Baseball Academy Stadium, where the Big Z played before the signing.

1997. He told me in January that the tryout was going to be in February. One day we went to his house and he told me, "There is an earlier tryout. The people from Chicago are in the stadium and want to see you play. Alberto Rondón wants to see you." I asked him when that was, and he replied that it was going to be the first or second week of February. I agreed. We kept training, and the day of the tryout arrived, but Alberto Rondón did not show up. I trained with them. The guy who watched me gave me an old ball and didn't show much interest in me. He asked me to throw some more balls and then told Julio, "This guy has a good arm but we don't know if it's going to develop. His mechanics are awful and he needs a lot of work. Nobody is going to sign him to go to the U.S." He did not even wait until Alberto Rondón, who was the person in charge, arrived to see me. Figueroa told me what had happened and told me not to worry, so we kept training.

The time came to go before the Toronto team. The person in charge in Venezuela was there, so were Julio and Pedro Ávila, who was the scout for Toronto. They were going to Puerto Cabello. There were about 27 guys. There were some baseball players who were going to be tested to see whether they would be signed. We got dressed and started running, and I was asked to pitch. I pitched about 85 to 86 mph.

What was your weight and height?

I was about 6′ or 6′1″ and 175 to 180 pounds. They chose other players and decided to send me to the academy in Barquisimeto. They told Julio, "We are only going to keep Zambrano. Send the others home. Could we go to Zambrano's house to meet his parents and get permission?" So they went with Julio to find out when they could take me to Barquisimeto. My brother Dennis was in the stadium. He went running home to tell my father they were coming. We left about 20 minutes later, and they talked to my parents. They told them that I had a good arm and that they wanted to take me to their academy. My parents agreed, and I was to show up there on Monday.

My father was then working in repairs and he arrived on Friday. I told my dad, "I have no clothes to go to Barquisimeto." His answer was, "I don't know if I am going to get paid today."

(In a later interview, Saulo recalled, "When he was signed, I felt so proud having a major league player in my family. When the news finally broke out, we jumped for joy. We happily screamed: El Toro was signed! There were only a few of us in the house celebrating because we were poor. I remember when he left for the United States and everyone gave him some money so he would have some. We could not go to the airport to say good-bye for we didn't have any money.")

What did you have to take with you?

Nothing. I had some shoes, although I used to say that shoes didn't matter. My brother Johnny arrived and said to me, "Don't worry. I'll give it to you." He gave me the money, and we went shopping at the open market on Saturday. I bought shoes, dress clothes, jeans, and two shirts. I left for Barquisimeto on Monday. We didn't practice until the next Saturday, when an American agent from Latin America for Toronto came over and I trained with him. There were about 50 baseball players, and they kept four for further interviews. I was the last one to be interviewed. They allowed my father and my brother to be present, but Julio told them, "I am the one who will be joining you." My father and my brother knew nothing about this business, and he was concerned they would be taken advantage of, so Julio asked them to let him be present and my father agreed. The gentleman said I was in good condition but I had to develop. Also, it was unknown if I would injure myself, so it was better to let me stay in the academy. Julio then firmly said, "If the boy does not sign today, I am taking him with me." Julio handled the negotiations as if he were my agent, so he asked, "How much are you offering to pay for him?" The gentleman told the translator, named Emilio, something in English, and he told us, "The gentleman is saying that he is offering $5,000 for signing." My brother Dennis jumped at him and said to Emilio, "Five thousand dollars? Are you crazy? For $5,000 I would do it myself. That's a new arm that hasn't pitched anywhere else." He got angry, and Julio told them, "We want $300,000 for him." They answered that they didn't know if I was going to be a good baseball player, and Julio responded, "Don't worry. We won't be working with you. We're leaving." They tried to persuade us not to leave, saying, "Don't leave like that. Let's at least sign him for the winter league with the Cardinals." Julio said to them, "You're wrong. I have seen this guy and I am the first one who wants him to be signed in the United States, and then to be signed here in Venezuela. I'll call Pedro Ávila." Then we left.

Later in the tryout for Florida, they didn't offer so much either. I went to a tryout with the Arizona Diamondbacks, who were just getting started at that time, and the scout told Julio, "That guy deserves good money, but we're just starting, and the money available is for the draft players. We can't give him that kind of money, but if I had it, I would pay it for him." His name was Carlos Porte.

We kept training. One day Julio came to me and asked, "Do you remember the Chicago chief, Alberto Rondón?" My answer was, "I never saw him so there's no way I could remember him." He continued, "Well, that guy is angry because everybody has seen you but him." I then realized that Alberto Rondón didn't know that I had been there, that the Chicago coaches had already seen me. Julio talked to him and gave him my phone number. When he called, I told him that we had already gone to them, and he got angry and threw a fit with the academy coaches. He apologized and asked to see me play. I had no problem with that, and Julio told me, "We got nothing to lose in trying to see if the guy finds something good in you." So Julio called him, and they agreed on a date. We continued training until the day of the second tryout with the Cubs and Alberto Rondón. He was looking for a fastball at 91 mph, but I didn't know that. That day I pitched right at 91 mph. My brother was watching the gun along with Rondón and Julio. He was the one to see it, and then Rondón saw it.

In a matter of months your velocity went up from 84 to 91 mph in that training process.

When I did the first tryout in Chicago, I was at 84 mph. With Toronto, I pitched at 86 or 87 [in February]. With Florida [in March] I pitched 84, 85, 86, and with Arizona [that same month] I pitched 85, 86. That was my velocity then. The people from Florida wanted to see me again in May. The person in charge called Julio, and he said, referring to me, "He looks good but is a little stiff; he needs some work." Julio responded, "I'm working with him every day." The scout insisted, telling Julio, "The boy is a little stiff, I don't know. I'll call you." We again left a tryout disappointed.

Did you talk to Ismari about that?

No.

IZ: I didn't even know he played baseball.

Big Z: She didn't know that I was training to be a professional because, at the time, we had just started dating and I had not talked to her parents yet. When I learned that I was coming to the United States, then I told her and she said that I had to talk to her father: "Because if you are going to the United States without talking to my father, then we are finished." That happened while I was looking for someone to sign me.

(We continue the discussion about the signing and hiring process.)

We kept on training, but I felt the weight of frustration because there were four teams already that didn't want to sign me. One afternoon we went out for a run in the same training area. After we ran, Julio was all smiles when he said, "Carlos, I have good news for you; the best news. I think there will be a signing tonight." "What happened?" I asked anxiously. "Rondón called and he was desperate. He wanted to see you again, to talk to you, to your mother and your father." We went to Julio's house to wait for him. He arrived in a beautiful Camry with nice wheels. He brought the coach who saw me in my first tryout with him, the one who didn't allow me to stay, and another coach. He told Julio, "I am going to tell you something. I am not going to offer you castles."

This was Rondón talking?

Yes, Rondón. He said, "I am going to be honest with you. I am not going to tell you that I am going to take you to the moon if I am not actually going to. I am going to let you stay in the academy for a month. If you develop in a month, I will take you to the United States, and you will be signed there. They will give the verdict. I need to talk to your parents, when can I talk to them?" My answer was, "They can go to the stadium to talk to you, if you want." He said, "That sounds good. In the meantime, I have a present for you." He gave me a right baseball glove and told me it was mine. He then reached for a uniform and said, "Welcome to the Chicago Cubs." I remember it was No. 21, and I was so happy. "I want you in the Academy early in the morning. Don't be late," he told me. I answered, "Don't worry. I'll be there tomorrow." When he left, we were so happy. When my parents and brothers heard the news, they could not be happier because I was going to be signed in Chicago. The next day, I went to the academy early in the morning. All those players knew exactly what do, where to pitch. I got dressed and got to work. I was there for about a month.

After a month, while having dinner at his house, the coach told me that I had to do a daily report and that "a scout who is in charge of Latin America for the Chicago Cubs is coming. His name is Oneri Fleita." He came to see me on May 22 and he asked me to pitch. The first pitch was against a guy who came from a Class AAA team, and his bat split. Oneri grabbed me by the shoulders and said to me, "Big and strong man," as if he did not speak Spanish. My brother-in-law was sitting in the audience. He did speak Spanish, I later found out that he was of Cuban descent. He started speaking to Alberto Rondón in English, but I didn't understand a word of it. "You need to get a passport because you are leaving for the United States the last day of this month," Rondón told me. I said, "If you will excuse me, Rondón, but my birthday is July 1. If you don't mind, I want to spend that day with my family." He agreed without hesitation. That same night, I went to visit Ismari, and my future brother-in-law was making fun of me. I told Ismari that I was going to the United States: "The American gentleman came today and told me I was going." She then said, "Then you have to talk to my father and tell him we are a couple." I did not know what to do, but I quickly decided to talk to him.

How long had you been together?

Almost a year.

I told my father-in-law, "Listen, Ismael, it's no secret that I like your daughter and I want to ask your permission to date her." He responded, "I have no problem as long as you respect her and we have a set time for you to come visit her." We talked, and everything was clear. After that I got my passport and my visa. I first came to the United States on July 7, 1997. I traveled with Alberto Rondón.

My first experience on a plane was unforgettable. I was not prepared for takeoff since I had never been on a plane before. Rondón looked at me and told me to calm down—I was really nervous. We landed in Miami, and I was just starring at everything. Rondón told me to hurry because we still had another plane to catch before we could reach our destination. We kept walking, and Rondón was walking fast while I was trying to keep up while carrying my suitcase. We went through customs and got to the departing gate. We were flying first class. My blood pressure went down and I started throwing up. I was given a bag and some pills, but I wasn't used to that. We finally arrived in Arizona.

The first person I saw seemed to me like a star. He greeted me and introduced himself as Franki Beltrán. They took me to get some rest. The following morning we went to the stadium, where I trained with them and I met the minor league coach. All I heard were whispers and people moving their heads up and down, like they were agreeing with one another. A few days later, Oneri Fleita called me. He told me he was the one who helped me leave Venezuela. I was surprised that he spoke Spanish. He delivered some great news: "We are going to sign you with Chicago today. The people in charge liked you, and we are going to sign you." On July 24, Vick Conner called me. He was the person in charge of the minor league. He asked me to go to his office to sign the contract. After I signed, I said, "Thank you, my Lord, now I am part of Chicago." They welcomed me to the Chicago Cubs, and this is when one stage ended and the odyssey started.

There is an anecdote that your brother Victor shared with me: Dusty Baker, manager of the Chicago Cubs at the time, was being interviewed, and they started asking him about pitchers Kerry Wood and Mark Prior. He said, "Why are you asking me about them? The greatest one is Carlos Zambrano."

What do you say to such expression, coming from someone like Dusty Baker?

Dusty Baker is a well-known person in baseball, not only as a manager but also as a player. I have seen videos of him playing, and he really has passion for the game. Maybe when I pitch, I remind him of himself and those times. I am very grateful for that comment, given that I come from Venezuela, from another culture, another language. It was difficult but, like I always say, God has a purpose for each person.

In this marvelous story, what do you think was the key to achieving and maintaining success?

I am going to honestly tell you the key: the first one is God.

In what sense?

I believed in God since the beginning. A few days before coming to the United States, I was at my pastor's house, and he told me he wanted to pray for me. He began praying, and God spoke to me some beautiful words: "I am with you; I am going to bless you in an astonishing way. I am going to lead you to things you cannot even imagine and I will be with you when you drift away. I will do things anew." I have believed in those words since then. I believe that this has been one of the keys to my success, believing in God, having the faith that He is going to lead me and nothing bad is going to happen, for He is with me.

The second tool is discipline. Since I started my career, I have been a very disciplined person. I like to learn. When I was playing in the minor leagues, some of my teammates were distracted, looking at women and other things, but I was never like that. I would watch my teammates and analyze their game, study the batters. I like to study—like when the Bible tells us that we need to scrutinize the scriptures. In baseball, we have to scrutinize the batters, analyze them, compare them, and learn from them. If a pitcher has more experience, I can learn something from him.

The third tool for success in my formative years was knowing how to listen to those who have knowledge.

Was there any other tool that may have been important for you in helping you stay firm?

I like to teach and learn. You can learn for yourself while teaching others.

Was there any baseball player or any other person who inspired you?

Wilson Álvarez from Venezuela and Roger Clemens from the U.S. They are people who I have followed since I was young, and I have always admired them.

(In December 2005 I visited Big Z and his family in Venezuela. While enjoying a delicious Venezuelan corn griddle cake known as arepas *in the kitchen at their apartment, I witnessed a significant event. All of a sudden, Ismari stood up and went looking for something in a small refrigerator in a corner of the kitchen. Carlos noticed that she was having trouble closing the refrigerator, so he tried to fix it. He tried many tricks until he finally succeeded, but not before succumbing to a burst of anger. He then came back to sit with us. Comparing that small refrigerator to the enormous stainless steel one at his home in Chicago that even had a television in it caught my attention because I remembered the Big Z's mom telling me that there were times when they didn't even have a refrigerator in the Cumboto II house. I asked the Big Z about that.)*

About two years after I signed as a professional, I told my mother, "In two years, I am going to move you from there." And it happened. Two years later, I was promoted to the major leagues, and I bought them a house in Cumboto I.

CHAPTER 4

FIRST STEPS

Carlos is not afraid of any batter.
—Julio Figueroa, about the Big Z, 2005

As part of my trip to Puerto Cabello in December 2005 and January 2006, I enjoyed one of the traditions that started with Carlos and his integration of sports and faith. It is a game celebrated every year for the last seven years between young people from Cumboto II and young people from the area where Ismari grew up. Big Z is faithful to this tradition. Leaving behind his status as a major league player, driving in his luxury Lincoln Navigator, we went to pick up the players from their humble streets in Cumboto II. It was remarkable watching this star drive, stop, get out of the car, greet, and joke with everyone as if he were just one of them. It never occurred to this man of God to detach himself from his origins—he has stayed true to his people and his roots. On one occasion, we visited a sports store to buy sporting goods and equipment for children in the community. When the store clerk offered him some shoes of a lesser quality for the children, Big Z returned them to the clerk and asked to buy the best brand possible.

I had agreed to meet Carlos and Julio in the park at the National Guard's military camp, precisely where the Big Z had organized a youth congress with the name "Conquering the City."

Julio Figueroa is now a pitching coach for the Chicago Cubs in Venezuela. He was an amateur pitcher and a member of the Venezuelan selection—and he's obviously a big sports fan.

According to Julio, the baseball organizations started coming to Venezuela, along with their academies, in the 1980s. The Houston Astros were the first to recruit baseball players from the region and, little by little, some of them became stars, like Bobby Abreu (Philadelphia Phillies), Freddy García (Chicago White Sox), and Johan Santana (Minnesota Twins). The Chicago Cubs arrived in the mid-1990s and settled in Puerto Cabello around 1997.

True to his word, Julio arrived before the game started. We introduced ourselves, hugged, and moved to a shaded area. Standing and facing the game, we talked about how the Big Z became a star.

What was your first impression when you first saw him pitch in a training session?

Julio Figueroa: We were about 90 to 110 feet away, and he threw the ball at me. He did it without much effort and with good velocity. When I placed him on a juvenile team, he did-n't pitch much because he didn't know how. Nevertheless, we trained in the afternoons. I worked a company job until 4:30 PM, so he would wait for me at my house, and we would go for a run on the hills.

On the hills?

To the small mountains. It's a section about several kilometers long, mostly going up until you reach the top, where the Solano Fort [a tourist attraction] is. Once we got there, we worked on pitching mechanics.

(Julio emphasizes that even though he trained with him and dedicated time to the Big Z's athletic development, he was not fully aware that he had so much potential. Julio helped Carlos

(above) Youth from Monte Horeb Church and Barrio Libertad. The Big Z has been organizing the traditional baseball game for the group since December 31, 1998.
(below) The Big Z during an at bat in the traditional Monte Horeb game, 2005.

just like he helped many others at that time, because he is a person of great humility and just enjoyed working with young people, whether or not they showed great promise.)

I'd be lying if I say that I knew Carlos was going to be a star. I simply helped him because I helped other people and I was engaged by his personality. I remember him running in jeans and school shoes. He had nothing else to wear at the time. His sports attire consisted of a sleeveless shirt and blue jeans shorts. He did not have running outfits. The first time he went out for a run, he was wearing blue jeans and shoes that had some heel and no socks. "Are you going to run wearing that?" I asked. And he replied, "This is what I wear for running."

What was your routine?

We did speed running for strengthening, then we did screening and pitching mechanics.

What did you do when you reached the top of the hill?

We ran from the bottom to the top to strengthen the legs, and then we worked on abs and did the complete baseball routine and pitching strategies, including how to lift the feet, move the arm, this and that. He was a fast learner.

Did he fight much?

No. Carlos has a vibrant personality on the mound because he doesn't like giving up runs and he doesn't like to lose. Carlos is a winner who can earn millions of dollars. However, he will always be a winner who does not love money, a person who loves the game, loves to win, and loves people.

When did you realize that he had true potential as a player?

While we were training, Pedro Ávila, a friend of mine and a Toronto scout, gave me a call. He asked me to organize a tryout, and so I did. I took a bunch of guys, including

Carlos, and Ávila was impressed by him. I told him that he was only 15 and wasn't yet available, that his movements were still rudimentary. That was the first time he got on the radar. The next was when he pitched at 91 mph. And that's when Ávila exclaimed, "Wow, that is a raw diamond!" That's basically when I came to know who Carlos was. I had been training with him for a short time, without any kind of professional interest, but I also didn't have enough experience to identify him as a prospect. On the streets, many people who knew amateur baseball used to make fun of us.

What would they say?

That I would be signed first before that "lunatic" because he didn't play baseball. Even worse, there was a rumor going around that, once he was signed and the Americans actually saw him, they ripped up the contract in his face because they thought he was crazy. But, of course, these were just rumors. I didn't take them seriously—they made me laugh.

Were you involved in the whole process from when he was identified as a prospect until the Cubs signed him?

We went to a tryout with the Toronto Blue Jays. They saw Carlos and invited him to a big tryout that took place in Barquisimeto, where the Toronto academy is located. I accompanied him. There were about 14 baseball players, and they all had American agents. The only one without an agent was Carlos. Except for me, who acted as his agent, he didn't know anybody. The other guys had agents because they already had some experience trying out for pro teams. But the best among them, no doubt about it, was Carlos. Even so, they didn't treat me with respect because I wasn't an agent. I was a nobody to them. They asked who his agent was, knowing that I was the one who had brought him there. I was offered $5,000 for Carlos to play, while two other players who had agents with them were offered $35,000 and

$40,000. Carlos was being offered $5,000 because he didn't have an agent. I have always believed that the real value of a player should be based on his abilities, not on the identity of his agent. Thank God that changed for Carlos later. I think it was a mistake on their part.

Did you reach an agreement?

We didn't. I told them that they were not even close to offering what I wanted. Then they asked if he was staying at their academy, to which I answered that he would continue training with me and that was it. We kept training quietly. Then the Chicago Cubs made a better offer and took him to the United States.

In that time, after he went to Toronto, did he attend any other tryout?

We had already gone to a tryout with the Arizona Diamondbacks when he was just starting. The Marlins saw him, and a supervisor wanted to see him, but we were already in Toronto. The supervisor then came to Venezuela and asked to see him. I didn't see any problem with that and agreed. We were offered $12,000, and I turned it down. That was that.

What did he say when you turned offers down?

Carlos is very disciplined and he lets you guide him. He knew that when I said something to him, I had a good reason. Thank God.

Was he respectful? (He answers with a firm yes.)

Carlos has always respected me. Even now, as a major league player who is on his way to stardom, he always respects my positions. We almost always agree. He trusts me.

So, after the Marlins, then came the Cubs.

First the Blue Jays, later the Marlins and Diamondbacks, and finally the Cubs, and he joined their academy. We held out for the best option to take him to the United States when he turned 16.

Was he not signed here in Puerto Cabello?

No. He was signed in the United States, once scouts and coaches there saw his potential. At that time, this kind of a transaction could be done. Chicago brought him to the United States and kept him there when they signed him.

For how much did he finally sign?

Carlos signed for $130,000.

So, if he had accepted the $5,000 before…

Can you imagine? I knew that the Big Z was a real prospect.

How long was it from the first tryout until Chicago signed him?

About six months, more or less.

It must have been a fast and intense time.

Yes. Carlos's evolution has been fast, and I believe that even he doesn't know himself the way I do, or see in himself what I see in terms of his baseball abilities. On one occasion, in front of some Americans, when Carlos was just playing in the minors, I told Tommy Miranda that Carlos was going to be better than Kerry Wood and Mark Prior. The Americans told me I was nuts and didn't know what I was talking about. I insisted that I knew Carlos and what he was and wasn't capable of. Later, my words became reality. Still, we have only seen half of what this guy can give. They haven't seen Carlos Zambrano's full potential yet.

What do you mean?

They still haven't seen Carlos Zambrano at 100 percent. They've maybe only seen half of what he can do. It isn't easy coming from a humble family and having nothing to suddenly gaining fame overnight. You have to be in that person's shoes to know how it feels. I don't even know myself, but I do know Carlos well enough know that it's not easy going from nothing to everything so fast. Suddenly you have a job and money to buy all the things you never had. At the same time,

The Big Z at bat during a game between the Toros and the Buffalos—he's the owner of both teams— a youth and adults local baseball league.

adjusting to a new lifestyle takes time, and it affects your ability to concentrate on the game. As he is able to make adjustments, we'll see an even better Carlos Zambrano. As he matures and focuses more, he will be much better.

(Talk of the Zambrano family's poverty reminds Julio of the house were he used to visit Big Z's brother.)

It was a rustic house, made out of wood. His parents, being poor and with so many children, took care of them. There was a television that his brother Dennis bought in Caracas when he played with me. There was no real furniture—instead of a sofa or chairs, they sat on junk tires. What I admire the most about Carlos is that, even though he has so much now, he is still the same person. He has changed for the better. I can guarantee that. He is a humble person.

How do you describe his discipline during training?

He works hard. He always listens. I am still surprised that he remembers the things I used to tell him. I used to say, "Carlos, when you have millions—because you will have millions—always be humble, try to help, and let others help you because that's the beauty of life. The moment will come when you will be able to buy whatever you want, but you cannot buy friendship, humility, happiness, or generosity. That is the most beautiful thing." I would also tell him that while being a pitcher is largely physical, he also has to develop his mental game. When someone pitches 95 to 97 mph, he has to work more and more in that area, which is what we always worked at.

How did you do that?

I talked to him about the good and the bad things that he would encounter—maybe more of the bad than the good—which is what he would find in the clubhouse or in a dugout with reporters and fans. I stressed that if you have a weak mind, you won't get anywhere in baseball.

What should he be careful about?

Aggressive people who talk trash, people who hurt the game, those who are only in it for themselves, who pay no attention to trainers, coaches, or other players. He can learn more from the bad than he ever will from the good. I tell him he should be careful with those who just want to flatter him, and he should keep his honest personality. Carlos is a guy who came from a house at the side of the road and was suddenly transplanted to Chicago, a whole new world.

He had his problems. He missed about five or six flights back to the U.S. because he simply didn't want to leave home again. When he was sent back down to the minors, he felt defeated. He came home for a visit and told me he didn't want to go back. He said, "I don't want to go there anymore. I do not want to go back to the United States. I don't want to play baseball." He had his low points where he would act like that.

(These expressions from Julio reveal an aspect of internal struggles, loneliness, and adjustment that the Big Z and many baseball players face when they leave their homes to face a culture and a country that in many ways can be more hostile. Once he joined the minors, the homesickness crept in, and Carlos, like so many players before him, struggled to stay positive.)

After he signed as a professional, he spent all year in the United States and came back to Venezuela in September. One time, they wanted to send him to a special program for draftees at the end of November. The date arrived, and I knew that he had to be in the United Stated by 6:00 AM. The next day, he called to tell me that his passport had been stolen, that his ticket was stolen, and that he had lost this and that. It was all a lie. He just didn't want to go. He finally admitted that.

(Big Z spoke with me about those difficult times: "There were moments when I didn't want to travel to the United States, in particular before the wedding in 1999. I was thinking about my family and friends. I didn't want to leave them. We had been together for my entire life, and we were very close. It

was not that things were going bad in the United States, I just didn't want to leave my people.

"I worked with that, and I just decided not to think about it. I tried to ignore my homesickness when it bothered me. I rejected any thoughts I had about my family and friends at home, but that just left me feeling even more lonely. I had friends [in the U.S.], but it wasn't the same. I would use any imaginable excuse—from losing my passport, to missing my flight—but deep down, I just didn't want to leave. It was a tough transition. I had to detach myself from my family and friends and mentally place myself in the United States. I even stopped using our family slang during the process.

"This changed a lot after I married Ismari and she came with me to the United States. However, each year up north was another year of missing experiences with my brothers. I missed the way we acted when we were together—our jokes, the way we teased our mother. After I got married, I could not bring my wife with me right away because she was not given a visa. In the first year of our marriage, we were apart for six months. It was very difficult to leave her for that long."

During all this, the Cubs' directors were having a hard time understanding the problems Carlos was having integrating himself into his new surroundings.)

Cubs' management said that he must be out of his mind. How could he want to give everything up and just go home? Nobody really knew anything about him. I would tell them about his life, that he was young and immature. I explained that it wasn't easy leaving the humble, poor place that he came from and suddenly going to the United States as a draftee. I told them these things so they would know why this was so hard for him. Even now, even with how much he is worth, Carlos still hasn't found himself. He doesn't know who he is, and that is something that he's learning.

What was he thinking? Why did he want so badly to come home?

He wanted to be back in his church. He wanted to be home with his family. He didn't know where he stood in the U.S. He was experiencing a lot of things he didn't understand, like culture shock, loneliness, being in love, and so much more. This is a business, not just a game, and he was a draftee. It's a difficult process. To this day, if I see him on television, he asks me if I saw him pitch and then we share ideas about his pitching.

(While we talk, we watch the game, where the Big Z just hit the ball out, over the fence.)

From your perspective as a pitcher and pitching coach, what are his main assets and liabilities?

The best thing that Carlos has is that he isn't afraid of any batter, I can assure you that. He doesn't have respect for anybody when they're on the field, and that's a good thing. Off the field, he is respectful of all the players, but on the field, he does whatever he has to do because he wants to win. I believe you are born with that; it can't be taught.

Carlos isn't afraid of anyone, he doesn't have respect for anybody when he's on the mound. His fastball has significant movement, and he throws well over 90 mph. That's not easy to hit. He has confidence in it, which makes it very uncomfortable for the batter. He's intimidating on the mound.

As far as any shortcomings, right now I think that he makes unnecessary pitches, particularly when the batter already has two strikes. He doesn't come down with his fastball, which is his most difficult pitch to hit. A fastball from Carlos, according to the experts, is one of the most difficult pitches to hit in the major leagues. Within the last four years, he has been the third-most effective pitcher, behind Pedro

Martínez from the Dominican Republic (Mets) and Johan Santana from Venezuela (Twins). However, in order to increase his durability and have a longer career in baseball, Carlos has to try to make fewer pitches per game; not do more than 120, with 110 being ideal. But it's hard.

He'll improve with time. He's driven and motivated, which is both good and bad. With all the adrenaline, he tends to throw his front elbow, and that makes his arm come out a little longer, and the ball has no direction towards the strike zone. That means that when he has a batter with two strikes, he wants to throw a fastball, but he lacks pinpoint control. He wants to throw the ball so hard to strike the batter out that he loses concentration. That's one of the things that he can improve. But he has all the qualities in the world to be a tremendous pitcher for many years. He is also a good hitter and, even with his size, he's a good runner.

He had a batting average of .300 in 2005.

The Big Z is a great athlete.

Do you think that Carlos is a person who wants to help his country?

Yes, yes, yes. We've talked about that. Knowing what is around you is a virtue, and an athlete has to beware of the people around him.

(We pause because Big Z has just hit a triple into the gap in left center field, approximately 330 feet.)

If it were up to him, he would always be here. He really likes being here in Puerto Cabello.

Do you feel that the Big Z adapted to the culture in Chicago?

He is a person who adapts to everything. He adapted to the American culture. Carlos is a very smart person.

And his English is good, too.

Yes, he learned English quickly. In the interview for the Cubs' magazine [*Vine Line*, Vol. 20 No. 11], Jim McArdle mentions that his English is superior. He's even acted as a translator for other Latino baseball players.

(For Julio, some of the keys that have helped the Big Z succeed in sports and in life are consistency and perseverance. He overcomes any obstacles to achieve the goals he has set for himself. To that end, Julio talks about a time when he and Big Z lived together while Carlos was in the minor leagues.)

In the United States, after playing Class A Short, he was to legally play in Class A Advanced because he had earned it. At that time, the minor leagues were divided into Rookie League, Class A Short, Class A, and Class A Advanced, but later on, after he finished his training, he was placed on Class AA. While already in Class AA and looking good, they decided to send him down to Class A Advanced. And then I learned that he was going to be demoted to Class A.

I didn't believe that could be true because Carlos was playing well in Class AA, and I knew that he was excited because he was in Class AA and doing well. Worried, I explained to Carlos the situation—I knew he would be upset, and I wanted to soften the blow so he would accept it without getting too discouraged. This was in his third year, I explained to him that it was a normal transaction between baseball divisions. He answered, "Hey, Julio, nobody demotes me; nobody will move me from here." I thought to myself that he was out of his mind. I don't know what happened later, but when the Class AA team started, that's where he was. Here he was, told he would continue to play Class AA and he would later be moved to down to Class A Advanced. But the moved never happened. He was the best pitcher in the first two months in the whole organization. And he was finally called up...to Class AAA!

That same year?

That same year. Can you imagine? He ended up pitching 134 innings in Class AA. He didn't play in the major leagues that year because he had knee surgery. It was a minor injury, and he played in the majors the following year.

(Carlos later told me that Lester Strode, the minor league pitching coach, had mentioned to him that Carlos would have to be demoted to Class A Advanced because it was part of the process, but that he would later be promoted. The Big Z objected to being sent down because he wanted a chance to show that he could do the work.

"I had to work harder to set aside my thoughts about my family," Carlos said. "That was one of the most memorable moments in my life, because going from Class A to Class AA is something that only a few achieve. I was hopeful at first, but later I was told that I was in the Class AA list and was going to be placed in Class A Advanced."

This occurred during the spring training process, when the rosters for the different teams are put together. It happened that, during training, the Big Z pitched 20 innings and allowed only one run. Naturally, he made the team, and Strode called him afterward to break the news to him and to congratulate him. Later on, he was in Class AA for two months and was promoted to Class AAA, where he had great numbers.)

Another important challenge that Carlos faced was when they wanted him to become a closing pitcher. In an obvious show of frustration, he told me that what he wanted was to play baseball and that he did not like the idea of not being able to start games.

(For the record, Carlos started his career in the big leagues as reliever. However, not only has he been the most consistent pitcher in the last five years for the Cubs, but the Baltimore

Orioles, during a trade negotiation, actually preferred him over Mark Prior, another great starting pitcher for the Cubs. This is an indication, Julio believes, that they see in the Big Z a strong person and athlete.)

For those who don't know him personally, what's the most important thing they can take from this book?

It's important for Americans to know where the Big Z comes from—his background, his beliefs. I believe he is a great ambassador from Venezuela to the world.

In Venezuela, there has been a revival, to use an evangelical word, of good players. Do you agree with this?

Yes, it's true. It hasn't happened before. The baseball academies have a lot to do with that revival. When the guys arrive in the United States, they already know how to play baseball. In the past, when they signed, they went on to learn the fundamentals while already competing in the United States, and that was very difficult because the Americans were more advanced. The academies play the summer leagues here in Venezuela. Sometimes there are up to three games per week. When they're in training, the players are learning the fundamentals. There is a routine. When I arrived in the U.S., I noticed that they do the same routine we do here in Venezuela. The only difference is the place, but the fundamentals are the same.

Do people in Chicago love the Big Z?

The people in the United States love him a lot, especially in the city of Chicago. The Big Z is a simple person who gives himself to everyone and gets along with the Chicago fans. They are like soul mates. I ask him: "Carlos, if Chicago offers you $10 million per season and the Yankees offer you $12 million, would you go?" He wants to live in Chicago because he's happy there. That is his preference, although he is aware that this is a business.

Do you compare him with other pitchers from Venezuela who are already stars?

In that respect, they have more experience than Carlos and they have what Carlos is lacking, in terms of control. Everyone says that Carlos lacks pinpoint control, but that's his way of pitching. He will gain some control, but he'll always be that way. Now, when he can control that a little, he'll be much better. In terms of physical condition, here in Venezuela, there is no pitcher who can equal him. He could play in the All-Star Game if he wanted. He is where he is based on his own merits, and the numbers show it. Although the pitchers for the All-Star Game are chosen by the managers, this year he was not chosen because he didn't have the numbers at the time. After the first half of the season, he did a better job.

Listening to you, someone who knows baseball well and also know this athlete's personality, I have no doubt that the Big Z will have 20 solid years in the major leagues, God willing.

He is ambitious, very smart, and has a good heart. A person like that is hard to find in life—and one with money is even rarer. Thank God for the Big Z from Venezuela.

CHAPTER 5

ARRIVAL IN THE BIG CITY

I belong in this place…if I could dominate Alex [Rodríguez]…I can pitch in the major leagues.
—The Big Z, 2002

This book isn't intended to exhaustively chronicle the Big Z's rise to the major leagues. However, Carlos's arrival in the big city of Chicago played a crucial role in his life, and it is well worth acknowledging.

Carlos and his friend Isaías Mercado sat for an interview in the Zambrano family home in Puerto Cabello. Isaías, a pastor and music minister, was the Big Z's first friend in Chicago. Here, Carlos talks about his experience leading up to his arrival in Chicago. It should be noted that Carlos Zambrano had two beginnings in the majors. The first one happened with very limited participation before he was sent down to Class AAA again, where he had an outstanding showing (see his 2001 statistics). The second time was to stay.

We had just finished dinner, and I suggested to Carlos and Isaías that we talk about his arrival in the major leagues. He is very busy whenever he's in Puerto Cabello, so we had to take advantage of every moment. On this occasion, on top of wanting to spend time with his friends and family, the Assemblies of God Churches Congress was taking place in Venezuela, in the state of Falcón. We met in his bedroom,

(above) Delivering a gift to National Guard Personel that helped in the Monte Horeb Youth Congress, organized by the Big Z, December 2005.
(left) The youth group of Monte Horeb, taken during an Assemblies of God National Church Congress on Punto Fijo, Estado Falcón, January 2006.

and without major distractions, the three of us all sat on the bed and talked about the time Isaías and Carlos first met.

Isaías recalls that Carlos asked the team's chaplain, Noel Castellanos, for help in finding a church in Chicago. Castellanos asked Isaías to help a young baseball player named Carlos Zambrano, who was going to be promoted.

Isaías Mercado: That was when he first gave me the phone number of the Hampton Inn he was staying at in Illinois. I called Carlos and went to pick him up. It was a Wednesday, if I'm not mistaken. I remember that I borrowed a car, a more comfortable car because my car was not working properly and I didn't want him to feel uncomfortable. I picked Carlos and Ismari up and took them to church.

(Carlos then commented about his arrival in Chicago.)

Big Z: I remember that the Director of Player Development/Latin American Operations, Oneri Fleita, and the Class AAA manager called me. In reality, the first time that I was sent up to the majors was not as exciting as the second time.

So you were sent up one time, sent down the second, and the second one was the charm?

I was sent up and down. After I pitched against Milwaukee, I lasted about 10 days in Class AAA. As a matter of fact, I believe that my wife stayed in Chicago that time. My locker was right beside Sammy Sosa's. When I saw his name next to mine, a beginner like me, who had just been in the major leagues for a few hours, next to someone like Sammy Sosa—who back then was very strong and his name was making more noise than that of Mark McGwire and Barry Bonds—can you imagine! He was very popular then.

(Laughs) I got to Chicago on a Sunday. I was in Iowa, and the team was in Arizona. I remember going to the hotel to check in, and when I tried to look up the game on the television, the hotel did not have that channel so I had to find a sports bar near the hotel to watch the game. The next day we had a double header.

You were watching a game with a team you were going to play on the next day. What thoughts did you have at that moment?

Big happiness. So many things crossed my mind while I pitched against the Milwaukee Brewers. As a matter of fact, when I was in Chicago, so many things crossed my mind—it was like a parade of events that had taken place, from growing up in Puerto Cabello to the signing. I often talk to myself, and I remember saying, "Carlos Zambrano, here you are, and all you have left to do is to ride this horse."

(Big Z began his career in the rookie league, where he played for a year, then another year in Class A. From there, he was promoted to Class AA, where he stayed—against the manager's will—with a 1.35 ERA, which made him their best pitcher.)

When I arrived in Wrigley Field, I received a call from the director of the minor league, who told me, "The first game is tomorrow at this time, but you cannot play in the first game because you are not on the roster yet. You should arrive around the seventh inning." And that is what happened. When I arrived, they were in the sixth inning, so I put down my bag, greeted all the people who had seen me in spring training, and I was given my uniform. I was assigned No. 38.

Did you request it?

No. In the minors, I was No. 67. When I was assigned No. 38 in the majors, I didn't want to change it, so I decided that it was going to be my number for the rest of my career in the big leagues. John Lieber pitched the first game, and I believe Chicago won. After the first game was over, everyone came in. There was Sammy [Sosa] coming to get some rest and get ready for the second game, and also several other players. Everyone was very nice to me. I greeted them and was so excited to be in a major league clubhouse. The pitching coach then came in to welcome me.

How did the pitchers welcome you?

Very well.

How was that first experience with the pitching coach?

(He smiles like someone who does not want to tell the whole truth, but he is going to talk about it even when he is not very happy about it. He is going to find the positive side, like he tends to do with everything.) Let me tell you something, he was harsh with me, very, very harsh. He was the kind of person who likes to scold. No matter who you were, he would tell you off to your face, and sometimes he would treat people as if they were worthless. I think he did it because he would see potential in a guy, and that was his style. That is one of the things that helped me because I like challenges. When I cannot jump something, I try harder. If I am running a 100-meter hurdle and I can't jump an obstacle, I do everything I can to jump it...until I achieve it.

(Isaías interrupts.)

IM: I saw the difference in Carlos's life on a specific day. It was the day he pitched against the Texas Rangers.

(Tommy Miranda, the Big Z's agent and friend, told me about that day in an earlier interview.

TM: During the first round of interleague games in 2002, the Cubs played against the Texas Rangers. In that game, the Big Z was pitching against stars like Iván and Alex Rodríguez. He was in the game as a reliever, and he went up against Iván. He threw an inside sinker, but since Iván is strong, he muscled a weak hit into center field. Then Big Z took the count on Alex to 3–0 and threw a very hard fastball, and Iván was thrown out trying to steal second. The Big Z then struck out Alex, and striking out one of the best players in the game gave him lots of confidence. At the end of the game, Iván approached Big Z and told him, "Don't pitch to me like that anymore, you're going to break my fingers."

That was the day when Carlos said, "I belong in this place. If I could dominate Alex, I can pitch in the major leagues."

But his first year on the Cubs was not what anybody would have hoped for. He did not surprise anyone at all.)

Big Z: I had no experience and did not know the batters. However, I always survived. I started one or two games and was the reliever in the rest, until a week before the All-Star Game in 2002.

(Tommy Miranda told me that, when the Big Z was promoted to the major leagues, he had to compete with Juan Cruz for a spot in the starters' rotation. Cruz is a good pitcher from the Dominican Republic, a minister's son who had a great game in the competition. In fact, he ended the year with a 3–1 record and a 3.22 ERA. Carlos was frustrated when he lost the chance—even more since he believed, as many do, that you only have one chance to make it into the big circus. He was then promoted to reliever since he was lacking the number of pitches to be a starter. The interesting thing is that, what sometimes seems impossible to us, is possible for God.)

Big Z: 2001 was a historic year for me because I made it to the major leagues by God's grace. I can tell people, "I was in the major leagues!" My daughters can tell my future grandchildren that I was in the major leagues. To God be the glory, I went as far as He wanted me to go. Be it a single game or a 20-year career, I will be here as long as God wants me here.

How did you feel as a reliever?

Well, I always felt bad as a reliever. As I told you, I like challenges. I like to be in the midst of the game, watching the hitters, analyzing them. If not, I'm on the team's computers, checking out the batters or watching the game on television, which is where you can best grasp the pitching types. That's the way I am. I am hyperactive, dynamic, I like to pitch and run. I have always said that I want to be a player, a complete pitcher, one who steals bases and who can hit.

(The Big Z is the only pitcher in the history of the Chicago Cubs who has hit home runs from both sides of the plate in one season. His batting mark in 2005 was .300, something very unusual for a pitcher. In a recent interview for Vine Line *magazine, his friend and colleague, Aramis Ramirez, said, "He is always around there, watching the game and paying attention....He got his spikes on, just in case he is asked to pinch run or pinch hit. He is always in the game" (Vol. 20, No. 11; p.15). These comments from a colleague and friend confirm his perception of himself in the game.)*

That's why, when I'm offered the opportunity to touch the ball, I touch it; when I have the opportunity for a hit and run, I do it. I do anything that I can. People see me big and strong, and maybe they're afraid of playing offensive with me. I, on the other hand, I feel ashamed when I see [Greg] Maddux stealing a base. Each time that Maddux steals a base, I bow my head, because he is a 38-year-old man who's showing he's in better shape than I am. *(Laughs)*

(In the ninth inning against the New York Mets on July 15, 2006, the Big Z stole his first base in his career. After getting to first with a single, he stole second without a signal from the coach. At the end of the game, he was asked what his motivation had been: "It was Greg Maddux." Referring to that, Dusty Baker, his manager, said, "The guy is a ballplayer, he is not just a pitcher....He is a runner, he is a hitter, and he is a fielder. This guy comes to play.")

You move all right, for your weight and height. I have seen you running.

Thank God I am conditioning well. When I was training here in Venezuela, I did the 60 yards in seven seconds, which isn't bad for a heavy and big man like me.

You have to stop eating arepas.

(Laughs)

How was the competition to get a space in the rotation in 2002?

In 2002 Juan Cruz started well in the sense that he looked good, but he would lose games. He even had a record of 1–11 or 2–11, something like that, although with a low ERA.

(In total, he had a 3–11 record with 3.98 ERA in 45 games.)

Then they went to the bullpen to evaluate who was going to replace him in the rotation. The person choosing the pitchers needed one to start, so they decided to give me a second chance. In that game, I pitched five good innings against Atlanta, and they only scored two unearned runs. This time, I took advantage of my chance.

In 2002 you were in your first full season. You had a 4–8 record and were a reliever for half of the time and a starter for the other half. How did you feel during that season?

In the beginning I was a little confused; I wasn't settled in the major league and didn't have the necessary practice. I came to know what He wanted for my life, and one of the things that He wants for me is to be in the major leagues.

Referring to the cultural transition, it seems like your English is very good.

That was also something that God did, because when I was in the amateur league, I didn't attend English classes so often. The classes started at 4:00 in the afternoon, or sometimes at 2:00 or 3:00, and we were already tired at that time. I would fall asleep. Then there was a moment when I started asking how do you say this, how do you say that, and do you combine this verb with that other verb, and by asking questions, I learned. Like the old saying goes, "You get to Rome by asking." So I started asking and talking with Americans, with no fear. Every day, I tried to learn a new word. When I learned a new word, I repeated it many times until I mastered it.

You even taped a commercial in the United States.

With Chevy, for a van. I have already done several ads.

(Isaías interrupts.)

IM: Carlos is daring and he just goes and starts talking, and many times I have been with him when he asks how to say something. I then say a word. He learned because he was so daring.

Big Z: I like to learn, and what I don't know, I try to learn.

You come from a poor community in Venezuela, from Puerto Cabello, a city with a very important harbor and with one of the most important oil refineries. However, it's a community with serious economic limitations, like many other cities and towns in the world, including the United States. You then arrive in a big cosmopolitan city, one with global impact, and go to Wrigley Field, with a great baseball tradition and a very demanding fan base. How was that?

Regarding the fans, I remember one occasion when I struck out Richie Sexson when he played for Milwaukee. I was so excited that I did my usual aggressive gesture, but not against him because I respect him very much and he is a very quiet person and a friend of mine. It was a very important inning, and when I did the gesture, the fans, some 38,000 or 39,000 of them, stood up and started clapping and yelling. I got goose bumps! I went back to the dugout and all I could say was, "Wow!" It's impressive how people back you up and how people like that kind of thing. I think the Chicago fan likes action. This passion might be because they haven't won in so long. But they like that attitude and, from then on, I became more familiar with them and vice versa.

On a day-to-day basis, have you experienced discrimination because you are Hispanic?

The Big Z and Johan
Santana of the
Minnesota Twins
during the Baseball
Classic in Puerto Rico,
March 2006.

The Big Z dominates during
the first World Baseball Classic
in Puerto Rico, March 2006.

Not in my case, I have never really felt it. The Chicago audience has been very receptive with me and with Hispanics. In the beginning, when I first got to the majors, I felt like I was not a part of it. Everything seemed strange to me. Now, on the contrary, I go to Wrigley and I can walk around it with my eyes covered and I know where everything is. I am not going to trip over anything because I made that field and that city my second home.

(Saulo, his father, related an interesting incident that happened in Chicago with two policemen. "It was snowing when I left the apartment. I walked for a while until I got lost. A police car drove by and, although I do not speak English, I stopped them. I showed them my passport: "Friend, father, Carlos Zambrano." When they realized I was Carlos Zambrano's father, they were very excited and opened the door of their car to let me in. They started talking among themselves, for I did not understand what they were saying. They finally took me to

Carlos's apartment and asked the personnel at the apartment building if I was Carlos's father. They were very nice with me when they realized I was Carlos's father." He concludes by telling about when he sees somebody wearing a shirt with the last name Zambrano on it: "I get very emotional and feel like crying when I think how my son has made the name bigger. Seeing how far he has come fills me with pride.")

Speaking of how supportive the fans are of you, I can tell you that, at the game I attended against Houston, I saw many American fans wearing Zambrano T-shirts, as many as were wearing those of Mark Prior or Kerry Wood. Now, referring to your colleagues, did you feel discrimination from American or other Hispanic ballplayers?

In the beginning, there were pitchers who expressed racism against me, but I'm going to keep the names to myself. The only thing I do now is bless them.

Did they try to set obstacles against you?

Yes, they tried to make me look like the clown, they wanted to ridicule me in front of my peers by doing things that I did not want to do—and since I was a rookie, they thought that I would fall for those things. But I have always thought that rookies should be treated with respect.

Something interesting is that now, when you are approaching the dugout at the end of an inning, you point to the sky, and the Cubs fans do that too or look up trying to spot something. It is a rite already. When did you start making gestures worshipping God on the field?

It was during the times in the minors—I use it as a moment to worship God, who has given me everything, without me deserving anything.

Isaías, you were telling me some stories about when Carlos first came to Chicago. You told me something about a visit to the dentist...

IM: Once, he had to go to the dentist. We were the only family he knew there. Watching that huge man, so tall and big, squeezing himself in a two-door Toyota Tercel was very funny. After he had his molar taken our, we went downstairs in the elevator, and I was afraid that this enormous man was going to fall on me because he was so out of it. He doesn't even remember when he went back into the car. I reclined the back of the seat. His face was full of blood and he couldn't talk very well, so I drove him home to Ismari. He never admitted this, but every time I tried to say good-bye to leave, he would complain about the pain and ask me to stay with him.

Toro, is that true?

Big Z: Yes. *(Laughs)*

(At this time, their wives join the conversation, as well as their daughters.)

Chicago welcomed me with open arms. In fact, Chicago has always been receptive with their draftees. I don't know about other teams because I have never played with any other team, so I can only speak about what I have seen in Chicago.

(Big Z's expression lights up with pride and thankfulness towards a city that has recognized and valued him.)

When we were in France and Spain on vacation, we saw some people from Chicago who were there on vacation, too. When they saw us, they exclaimed, "I love you, man....Oh, my God I cannot believe it." *(Laughs)* Also in Spain, a woman with her family yelled, "Carlos Zambrano, we love you." I believe this summarizes it. The people in Chicago are spectacular. *(He starts making gestures and sounds like a bull and everyone starts laughing.)*

We can affirm that Chicago has welcomed you well.

Yes, and not only me. I have also seen Ronny Cedeño and other draftees who have arrived in Chicago. The team had been expecting them and, when they walked in, everyone start clapping because the new players had already been in the newspapers. They are going to succeed. That is nice from the Chicago fans.

You are a very emotional person in the game. I was reading on the Internet an article from the 2004 season that said Zambrano "is working with his emotions." That goes with what you were just saying. Have you made adjustments in the way in which you deal with your emotions in the game? Do you get frustrated when something goes wrong?

Yes. I believe, that year after year, God has allowed me to learn to handle and control my emotions. I remember that in the early years, in 2001, I got a reputation with some batters—some were afraid of me and others were angry at me. Some did not like the way I pitched. Those early years I wanted to do more than the norm in order to stay and establish myself in the majors. In that sense, being so emotional sometimes does not agree with other players, and naturally, with the opposing team. In 2002 I improved. This is when I had the problem with Barry Bonds. Many things were said, like that I was disrespectful to him. I remember an article from 2004 that said that the Cubs didn't want me to lose my passion that had helped me win 13 games in the previous year as their fourth starter. But neither did they want me to lose control and lose concentration, a balance very hard to find. To this, my pitching coach said: "I like that fire, but keep it under control."

The Incident with Barry Bonds

Tell us about that experience with Barry Bonds.

It was 2002. There were three men on base, and I was acting like a rookie back then...*[More than rookie behavior, these are character traits. In the evening of April 24,*

2006, while he was pitching against the Florida Marlins at Wrigley Field, Carlos stepped to the plate. In his second turn at bat, he struck out with two balls and two strikes. In his frustration, he broke the bat with his right thigh. Surprisingly, the fans started clapping. He finished with no decision, but he struck out 12 in 7 innings—and the Cubs won the game 6–3.]

There were two outs, and I pitched Barry Bonds a fastball. He hit a slow ground ball toward my hands for the third out. I was so very excited and I screamed. Can you imagine? I had subdued "the biggest one." I then made some emotional gestures, not to him, but to myself—gestures showing the excitement of having subdued a big man in baseball. I thought, "Wow, how could I have subdued Barry Bonds?" But he didn't see it that way because he had reached for the bat and gone back to the dugout. However, some reporters started to sow discord over my actions. I kept on walking and threw the ball at the audience. That is what made him angry. He was told later that I had disrespected him. That is what the reporters told him, so he replied, "If he did that, I have to see it." I believe that he later saw the video and the next day he publicly declared that he was going to teach me how to be respectful, that he was going to teach me how to conduct myself in the major leagues and that nobody could do something like that to him. He said he would get me and teach me respect, meaning he was going to hit a home run. Until now, it hasn't happened during the season, thank God.

In spring training, he homered one once, but that doesn't count. I'll tell you something, if he hits a home run during the regular season and he just stands there or runs backwards to show disrespect towards me, I would just clap—he's Barry Bonds. If someone else scores, maybe I'll get

The Big Z's outbursts of emotion on the field are often aimed more at himself than at opposing players.

angry, but if it's Bonds, that might take me to the record book. Maybe I'll be the pitcher who allows the record home run. *(Now, Bonds is the new home run king, having surpassed Hank Aaron's record of 755 in August 2007.)* You're not always in the record books because of what you've done, but sometimes it's because of someone else. *(Laughs)* These are the things you learn from your experiences in the majors, which make you better. I have already been through many situations, and I believe I've improved.

Before that problem got resolved, two years after this happened, we met each other again in the 2004 All-Star Game. I prepared for the All-Star Game and, to my surprise, there was Barry Bonds. I remember that when I went into the dressing room, he was beside Carlos Beltrán [centerfielder for the Houston Astros then, now with the New York Mets] and Eric Gagne [reliever for the Los Angeles Dodgers, now with the Boston Red Sox]. I was there, minding my own business. I went in to change, and I saw him come in. I told myself, "Here is this guy, and maybe he is coming to say something to me." I continued getting dressed. He went to his locker and did something and then started talking to his coach for about 15 minutes. I kept getting ready and looked with the corner of my eye when I noticed that he was approaching me. When I saw him coming toward me, I told myself: "Well, if this guy comes to talk to me or gets nasty with me or insults me, I'll have to slap him just once and there will be big trouble. I am not more or less of a man than anybody else, but we are going to have a problem." I made a fist with my left hand and thought, "He is coming on the right side, so I cannot just use my elbow, but I can bend over and at least throw a punch."

The man approached me and put his hand on my shoulder and greeted me, "Hi, how are you?" I answered, "Good, thanks to God, how about you?" He then said, "You know what? Whatever happened in the past, should stay in the past. What happens in the game field should stay in the game field. Sometimes we want to do so much on the field and I know you are a talented young man and you will be very big." He continued talking to me so nicely that I felt ashamed because I thought that Barry Bonds was a despot who liked to undervalue people and belittle people. That was his reputation because he is big in baseball. But I realized that it was the opposite. Barry Bonds is a very gracious person, who makes mistakes like everyone else, but is not a pretentious person and has a good heart. I realized that he has feelings because when he said those words, I could not believe that he could say all that. He told me, "You know that we have to be united, all Hispanics and African Americans. We have to be together." I then answered, "I offer you an apology because I got too excited on account of me being a rookie." He replied, "Don't worry about that."

I realized his humanity in that moment. He has feelings like everyone else, and that is difficult when you have such a reputation. Everyone knows Barry Bonds, and that is hard to deal with. When you don't have people around you to help you deal with that and tell you what you are doing wrong, it is harder. Your friends are those who tell you things like they really are. When you're someone who's famous, you need to have someone who can tell you right from wrong, who can stay honest with you. That's the type of person he is, that's what he does. The man is the opposite of what I had been told and what I had heard. Well, after this meeting, we became friends. We spent the day playing jokes. Isaías was astounded because I was hanging out with Barry Bonds. Frank Álvarez, my assistant and personal trainer in Chicago, was also surprised because I spent the whole All-Star Game with him. He even offered me a ride in his limousine. Frank came with me, and it was a very nice experience. Being with all those people is a great privilege, sharing with Barry Bonds, Roger Clemens. I was like a kid with a new toy.

And among equals, because you were equals.

I believe we were among equals because we all had a jersey that read "National League." We were all wearing the same uniform, and that was the important thing. Everyone behaved like professionals, which is what we are.

You mentioned that when Barry Bonds approached, he gave you some advice. Do you remember what he told you?

Among other things, to always keep pitching well and studying the batters and to try to stay healthy. Also to try to train hard because, he said, I had the potential to be in the Hall of Fame. And to be humble, which was the most important thing and what people like the most about the players.

(The Big Z honors his family name through his display of emotions in the game, as well as with his desire to win. Yormis

remembers a story that frames this truth in an experience prior to a game against the Houston Astros.)

Yormis Zambrano: We were at a restaurant eating lunch and he said, "I can't stand the pain anymore. I have to go to the training room to put something on it." Willy Taveras was the centerfielder for the Houston Astros, now with the Colorado Rockies. He said that they would take him and, if he did not feel well, he should not pitch that day: "No, let's go and take care of his back." He left, and Tommy, myself, and three other people stayed. Frank Álvarez was there, and everyone was asking me how I saw Carlos. "I grew up with him and I know him well," I told them. "So if he complains of pain, he must be in real pain." Tommy then said, "I'm worried about Carlos. He's told me that he's a warrior, and I'm worried that if he goes on to pitch today, it could be worse for his career. It's better for him to lose a turn than to lose his career." I agreed to that, but "no one is going to get him out of there."

We arrived in the stadium, and I took his suitcase to him. He was in the clubhouse and just had something applied to his back. I gave him the suitcase and asked him how he was feeling. "It hurts a little," he said. "Then don't pitch today," I advised him. "No, I am a warrior," he insisted. "No one is going to get me out of here...nobody."

(He is a warrior and stubborn at the same time.)

We then went to a shopping center in Houston, and Tommy was worried about the situation all afternoon. At the beginning of the game, his pitching was between 96 and 97 mph. He looked well, and Tommy had said that, as he would warm up, he would feel better. He hit a home run, pitched eight innings, and struck out 10 players. Incredible. I told Tommy that they were lucky his back was hurting, otherwise they wouldn't have scored a single hit. At the end of the game and before I said good-bye (for I was returning to Venezuela), I told him, "You are a true warrior. A bull...my bull."

Fans, Family, Church Life, and Spirituality
Isaías, how was the Big Z developing spiritually while all this was going on?

IM: Obviously, Carlos already had a very solid Christian foundation. He wasn't a beginner in faith. He had some biblical concepts and theological thought. I was an associate pastor in Puertas de Alabanza [Doors of Worship] Church. Our friendship started there, along with that of our wives.

(A token of the unbreakable presence of God in the Big Z's life, Tommy Miranda tells us his earliest recollections of his relationship with Carlos. They met during the winter. He had requested that they meet at the church. Tommy was watching the service through a window. Later, Carlos confessed some of the parishioners were acting on his behalf because he, too, was watching through a window. Since then, they have maintained a friendship.)

How did the people at church receive you?

Big Z: In my church in Chicago, during the times I've been able to attend, people act normally around me. There are times when people act surprised and, when they see me, they open their eyes really wide.

How humble and presumptuous... (Laughs)

What happens is that, based on my experience as a fan, people look at you as if you were an alien. But I'm just a regular person like you, like Isaías, so I could never understand that. Once a fan, always a fan, and many times, whether they want to or not, the fan comes out. I have had that experience myself. The Real Madrid soccer team came to Chicago, and, when I saw the Real Madrid players, I was on cloud nine. That must be the kind of feeling my fans have when they see me. Real Madrid has always been my favorite team. My wife and I once went to a private dinner with Roberto Carlos and Ronaldo, and she told me, "When people see you, they act the same way you are acting now, so that's why you can't judge others." I then understood the fans' reactions. Before that, I couldn't understand it. I couldn't get used to it. When I go to church here in Venezuela, people act normally around me, like with any other church member, because they are used to seeing me around.

IM: In the church in Chicago, people react by trying to give helpful advice. People tell me, "Please, Isaías, talk to Carlos and tell him to calm down, to not get so angry." I would tell them no. Carlos is a man and he has to make that decision. I believe I have said something to him once or twice, between him and me, about the fans asking me to talk to him. Carlos Zambrano is his emotions. We cannot forget that his passion is what he does. The day when Carlos abandons all that passion, he would stop being himself because his passionate love of the game keeps him motivated. It keeps him going. He pushes himself, he challenges himself, and he corrects himself on the mound. We see him yelling and, many times, he's yelling at himself. Last year I found out that he would tell himself, "Charlie, what is going on, Charlie?" He was yelling at himself. I would tell people, "Please let him play. He is a grown man and he will find himself and then he will connect." They do it out of appreciation and because they identify with him.

Isaías, how have you felt being a pastor to this man who is hard to tell whether he is a sheep or a goat? How do you define the experience of being a pastor to the Big Z in Chicago? If you want, we can ask him to leave the room.

(*Laughs*) I may have a different style of being a pastor. I don't believe that I have been for him a pastor as much as I

The Big Z reacts as a fan with his own sports idol, Roberto Carlos, soccer star from the Real Madrid and Brazil National Teams.

have allowed our friendship to be the vehicle through which we talk about certain things and, as a result, grow spiritually. I believe that when he entered the majors, Carlos's personality began a difficult transition—he was challenged to stay true to himself spiritually because he was being exposed to a new world, facing challenges he never saw before. Under those circumstances, keeping that spirituality alive would be a challenge for any of us. I could see that was what was going on with Carlos, that he was being challenged to maintain a healthy and vibrant spiritual life.

How do you describe the process from 2001 through today?

Carlos came to Chicago as a believer in 2001 and he always looked all right. He came with biblical principles and a solid foundation. I saw him as a very wise person who obviously had a temper. But those things don't surprise me, for I am also a man and at that age I had to go through certain things, too. So for me, facing spiritual challenges was normal. Now, last year, I noticed a change in him. I think I told him at the beginning of the year, "Carlos, I don't see you at peace when you're on the mound. I do not know why that is, but I am praying for you. I love you very much." In that particular moment, I felt that I had to remind him to look for God's peace.

How did you receive those words from Isaías as a friend and pastor? When he says such things, how do you handle it? Is it something you easily accept?

Big Z: When someone gives me advice, I accept it, whether it is easy to listen to or not. There is a very important text in the Bible that says that we have to scrutinize everything, listen to everything, keep the good, and reject the bad. The human being is like a word processor. You receive information and grasp it. But this information is like when a person is working at an apple orchard. You have to pick the good apples and throw away the bad ones. The human being is just like that. We should listen and retain the good from a conversation or a relationship or a friendship; keep the good, reject the bad.

I'm not saying that Isaías gives me bad advice. I obviously receive all the advice that he offers me. However, we have had our differences—especially as we study the Bible, we don't always agree. But that's normal when you are sharing about the Bible and ministry—it's a discussion, not a debate. Talking to pastors and people who have studied the Bible helps you to learn more, to have more knowledge. In talking with people who have more knowledge than we do, we learn a lot. It's better for me because, when I go into ministry full-time, I will already have some information, a series of experiences that I have lived through that made me stronger and wiser.

How do you define spirituality?

I believe spirituality is to scrutinize the scriptures and to hold fast to God, to read and live His word every day and let it guide us. I believe spirituality is getting involved with God. After that, I believe that the Holy Spirit itself gives testimony to us. I think that the spiritual person should obey the rules, the commandments that have been established not only in the Bible, but we also have laws that should be observed. If you run a red light, for example, you are violating the law. In that sense, violating the divine laws can damage many things in our lives. So we should be careful as Christians and as human beings, and be careful with what we think, do, and say. Living a spiritual life mandates that you live by the commandments established in the Bible and the human laws. But there is another important dimension about spirituality that has to do with human relationships. In Galatians 5, for example, the fruits of the spirit are joy, peace, patience, kindness, generosity, faithfulness, gentleness, and self-control, and everything else you want to add to that is part of the love. That fruit of the spirit is directed toward the neighbor.

Who is your neighbor?

Everyone around me, my brothers, my friends, the people we know, and those we don't know.

IM: One of the ways in which I have observed Carlos and his desire to cultivate his spirituality is through the devotional times when he comes to our house and I play my guitar. I have come to understand that those moments, even lasting only for 15 or 20 minutes, are a worship service for Carlos. His liturgy happens at that time. I have talked about this with my family so, when Carlos comes over, I, as a pastor, can provide an atmosphere for him where he can talk to God. During our time of worship at home, there are elements of the liturgy, like prayers and praise, but also a lot of laughs.

I remember one day when we were in the car and suddenly Carlos popped a CD in. We both started crying. It was a time with God. I then understood that, as a pastor and a friend, I have to make sure that those times happen in Carlos's life when he comes to my house, since he isn't always able to attend the worship service every Sunday or Wednesday.

The Big Z climbs Venezuela's medanos (sand dunes) during a family trip, holding two of his daughters, Catherine and Carla.

The Zambrano family: Carlos, Ismari, Carlis, Catherine, and Carla.

A proud father kisses the youngest of his three beauties.

When he arrives, I get my guitar, and we have our time of worship with devotions. He shares the scriptures. I believe he is going to be a preacher, a minister of God. I think it is very important for people to know that this is a way in which Carlos keeps his spiritual life, through worship and praise.

(During our conversation about spirituality, the subject about the girls comes to my mind. Carlos has three beautiful daughters, and in them we can comprehend God's creation. While I tell this to the Big Z, his eyes shine while he gets ready to talk about the emotions of their births.)

Big Z: I first met Carlis, the firstborn, when she was 15 days old because I hadn't finished the Instructional League in Arizona. When we had Catherine and Carla, these were also very emotional times. The second child was born in Chicago, and the third in Venezuela in December of last year. Those were very special moments. I try to spend as much time as possible with them.

When I am home, I want to play with them. Many times, since they see me as being so big, they want me to give them piggy-back rides. They see me and say, "Daddy, pony." When I have a day off and am going from one city to another, I try to stop by Chicago and then go to wherever I need to go. When it isn't too far away, like St. Louis or Cincinnati, or even Milwaukee, I take them with me. I try to spend those time in nearby cities with them.

(Isaías shared that the oldest one can already recognize her dad at the mound on television. When seeing him, she exclaims, "Look at my daddy." She then runs to the television and kisses it, saying, "Daddy, I love you." Carlos was surprised because he had not heard about that.

One of the things that Carlos mentioned is that there were more downs than ups in his spirituality, particularly in 2004.)

In those moments, Isaías, how did you intervene as a pastor,
and how did he handle those fragile times?

IM: As a pastor, maybe I did not do so much. Being his
friend was more important to me. I didn't want to play a pastoral role because I consider myself his friend.

I tried to help him stay connected, but I did see those spiritual lows. It wasn't surprising, but with him, you worry
more because of the temptations around him. So I always
had people praying for him. Nobody can tell me that they
have not experienced spiritual downheartedness. Nobody can
tell me that they have never had times in which they did not
feel like praying. On occasion, you feel like just getting in
bed and going to sleep, but that is when God rewards the
believer: in your honesty. Those are stages in which you can
be aware of how far can you go. We all have a limit. That is
why many people steer away from God and, when they open
their eyes and awaken, they are so far away from God
because they have diverted their attention from their spiritual lives. They don't pay attention to what God wants for
them, to what God has for them. To me, this is called maturity. That is the maturation process. I think we all go through
this.

Later in 2005 I saw an awakening in Carlos that I have
not seen before. You could see it in the way he talked and the
way in which he saw life. Like me, he comes from a more
conservative tradition.

Conservative in what way?

A conservative Pentecostal tradition. When you look in
other places, you can widen your theological perspective as
well as your spiritual life. Carlos was also developing spiritually, growing and loving and appreciating the life that many
times the mechanism of the conservative churches does not
allow you to celebrate.

Nora with one of her granddaughters, Big Z's and Ismari's pride.

(Carlos begins to change positions as if he is getting ready to say something. His eyes light up as they do each time he talks about what God has done in his life.)

Big Z: When I think about that time [in 2004], I can see that my impulsiveness deepens when I am on not-so-good terms with God. When I am with Him, I let my spirituality flow and I let God work on me and set aside my impulsiveness. Like all human beings, when something bad happens, you feel like taking justice into your own hands. That is when Jesus's love comes into your heart and the Holy Spirit takes control, making you recognize your error and ask forgiveness.

I told the Almighty, "The day when I decide to find you, the day when I decide to follow a ministry, I do not want it to be for two or three days and then go back to how I was before. I want it to last for the rest of my life." That is the process in which I am right now…until His second coming. Thanks to Him, I am a youth pastor here in Venezuela. Tomorrow I might be somewhere else because he wants me doing ministry in the United States. Why? Because when the ministry comes from God—you don't decide where you are going, but He places you where there is a need. Why would you be in Venezuela where you are not needed just because you want to be there rather than being in India or China, if God needs you there?

The ministry consists of doing His will and following Him wherever He needs me. Would He want me in Puerto Rico? Would He want me in Venezuela? That is what you need to find in your ministry…God's perfect will.

IM: When you talked about the signs of maturity in his spiritual life, I remembered moments when he would call me and ask me to go to the road games with him. Sometimes I couldn't go, but I remember that one day he asked to see me just to talk about the Bible and pray. I knew that I had a pastoral role right then. We prayed and cried together. I have shared sermons with him, and those are indicators of his desire to develop his spiritual life. When we returned to Chicago, we went to a bookstore where he bought Bibles for his youth committee in Venezuela, and he was very excited for that new role.

Baseball is one of the vehicles that God is using now, but the Big Z will be a servant of God for the rest of his life.

(I talked to Carlos, and we discussed how, at the end of his career, he will be relatively young, around 40.) You are a youth pastor. What do you do in this new role at the church?

We are currently meeting with young people and looking for different kinds of activities that would allow them to develop spiritually. We celebrate with concerts, retreats, and Bible studies. "Conquering the City" is our slogan, and our goal is to introduce people to a model of Christ that isn't boring but a Christ who wants to save souls. We want to go spread the Good News everywhere. The Bible instructs us to go, preach, and baptize. We all have to do that as Christians. That is our mission. One of our main missions is to spread the Good News, and that is what we are doing. Next year, we will be going on more trips around Venezuela with Tommy, and we are hoping to bring some other Christian baseball players, too, like Albert Pujols and Carlos Beltrán, among others.

CHAPTER 6

THE BALL, THE BAT, AND THE GLOVE

EIGHT TOOLS FOR LEADERS ON AND OFF THE FIELD

There have been key elements that have guided the Big Z to God's blessing. Although each walk is different, we can always learn from those who have followed the Lord. We can use the tools others have used to guide our own lives toward the revival of Christ's gifts and so we can live our lives in spiritual reflection and contribute to a better society. We hope this chapter helps leaders inside and outside of the church, coaches and trainers of any sports, or simply people who want to reach personal greatness. The keys here can be discussed in group meetings in order to be applied in the life of the person receiving the teachings. Likewise, sports leaders can use this chapter to raise athletes' potential or those who want to use sports as a tool for blessing, using the Big Z as a model.

I. We can have God in first place in our lives.

The Big Z shows a clear conscience that we can place God first in our lives. This does not happen by chance and is not a matter of religion. It is the convincing expression of a person who is grateful for all the things that God has done in his or her life. This principle is fundamental in the life of the Big Z, and it does not happen by accident. It is indeed the result of a strong Christian education and of the conscious struggles that need to happen in order for something positive to occur.

Some religious leaders among the Pharisees in Jesus's days saw the opportunity to discredit him, so they asked him which one was the most important commandment. It is important to point out that the scriptures in Israel contain more than five hundred commandments and other instructions, so it was not an easy question. Jesus responded with the great wisdom that only the Holy Spirit can offer: "You shall love the Lord your God with all your heart, and with all your soul, and with all your mind." (Matthew 22:37)

Carlos is aware that everything he has comes from God, so before he starts pitching, he entrusts himself to God. After each inning, good or bad, he points to the sky, showing his gratitude to the Lord.

I think that for those who enjoy sports as a profession, this is only part of life. An instrument for something: money, recognition, a family, and many more things. All these things are not really bad. But the key to success in life, which is more than winning a game or breaking a record, and definitely more than mere training, is to recognize that there is something bigger than us, which is God and all his manifestations. The Big Z primarily recognizes that God is revealed in Christ as the reason for all things. We can make Him the reason for our lives by filling ourselves with His grace and putting love first in our lives. If we do not have love in our lives, any other sign is worthless.

II. We can learn to listen to advice coming from those who have more experience and set aside the bad.
Though he is a strong and temperamental person, Carlos has always been, since his beginnings, a person who listened to those above him, especially those who could teach him

how to personally improve. Julio Figueroa tells us that the Big Z was very obedient and disciplined when training. Carlos himself points that out as the second tool he used to achieve a place on the Cubs. Undoubtedly, he has known how to listen to others who have something worthy to say, and how to ignore the voices of those who were underestimating him or did not see any possibilities for success.

The apostle Paul shares in his epistle that we should scrutinize everything and keep the good things. That is, we should examine what is said to us or what we read, and at the end, choose what has good meaning for our lives. However, our social system drives us, men in particular, to react or defend ourselves instead of listening carefully before expressing our position. In a world where the impulsiveness and the energy of the young are glorified, we need to remember that there is no substitute for experience, and this is obtained with time, opportunities, and failures. Even today, the Big Z needs to grow and learn more about baseball, about God, about life. There is no doubt he has a promising future, because he knows how to listen, he can separate the good advice from the bad. Remember that God, for some wise reason, gave us one mouth to speak and two ears to listen. Carlos tells us that he had trainers with styles that were focused on negative things. But he knew how to capitalize from those difficult times and not focus on the needs but in the opportunities that would arrive. He also models the importance of listening to ourselves, remembering that the Holy Spirit walks with us at all times.

We can appreciate this during his stay in the minors. When the executives of the organization had decided that he was to stay in Class AA, he struggled with their low expectations of him because he knew that he was to be on the top, that's what he was feeling inside, what God was

(above) Big Z and Ismari with Puerto Rican Christian singer Samuel Hernández, November 2005.

(left) The Big Z loves his family, his team, and his new hometown. He's used God's gifts to make a name for himself, to help his neighbors, and to praise Him.

telling him. He felt it deep inside and he expressed it. And it all came true.

III. When training in any discipline, we can work our body, emotions, character, and spirit in a holistic way.

We have seen that the Big Z's trainer was by him in his spiritual development, especially thanks to the ministry of the Royal Rangers. The ages between 15 and 17 years old were a crucial period in his life. The apostle Paul emphasizes that our body is the body of Christ. He also expresses that we should present our bodies as a sacrifice of true worship.

Positive and successful growth and maturity, especially during the formative years, depend on integrating our minds, bodies, and spirits, without separating these aspects of our lives and just hoping we'll succeed. This is a very important truth when developing any area of our lives, personally or professionally. The Big Z and Julio knew the importance of this and incorporated it at all times in their process, working on both physical and spiritual development. For Carlos, everything has to do with God, his emotions and passions, well channeled, have an end: praising the glory of God.

IV. We can accept that the revelation of God's purpose in our lives is progressive.

When asking Carlos if, when he arrived in the majors, he had a desire to go back to Venezuela, he answered that when he got there, he was able to understand God's purpose for his life. After a struggle that began in the forgotten streets of Cumboto II, with only his faith and will, seven years later he could look back and affirm that God had been with him all along. The apostle Paul affirms that the human being was created by God with a purpose. However, we know that some people go through life without a defined purpose. We will always be good for something. On occasion, we waste our energy not recognizing that our life becomes more harmonious when we let Christ work through us and that He always walks with us, whether we want it or not, every single day of our lives.

V. We can always learn from negative experiences.
When facing negative experiences, Carlos did not give up, but he waited for the right time to reap rewards. He did not follow the bad path that would take him away from success. Remember that Big Z weathered many unpleasant moments when others may have given up. Being underestimated, struggling for assimilation in the United States, competing with Cruz for the last spot in the rotation, experiencing multiple rejections, and overcoming all the other obstacles that aren't mentioned in these pages were all part of the Big Z's success today. It doesn't matter what life brings us, as long as we can benefit from it. If we live believing that all things happen for a reason—for a good reason—like the Big Z, we'll see that we are instruments of someone who is above us and has chosen a more abundant path. In this way, he shows that the negatives are necessary.

The 2007 season has been a good example of Big Z's ups and downs and how he's been dealing with it, even making mistakes in the process. The Big Z had a rough start, fighting with a teammate, ex-Cub Michael Barrett. After that incident, he apologized, then focused on the so-called "new season" that led him to be named National League Player of the month in July (5–1, 1.38 ERA). In August he held no victories at all, but he did finally sign his first multi-year contract. Later, in his first September appointment against the Dodgers, at Wrigley Field, he was hammered while the fans booed him. He didn't respond in a decent way, but labeled the fans as selfish—and many even retaliated by blaming him for the sudden slump in the battle for the Central Division. But once the heat of the moment had passed, he apologized again in a press conference and he got back on track.

Life has up and downs, and the Big Z's life speaks to that. He needs to improve while keeping the vibrant personality that has given him so much.

VI. Our personalities are part of what God uses to fulfill His plan.

God gave us our personalities, so we shouldn't change them just to please others. No one is worth changing God's pattern. We are too valuable for Him. Our life experiences shape us in His image. Some people, out of great love, may worry about Carlos's temper, but it's important to understand that he will change if God wants him to change—and God will be the only one who can and should do this. The Big Z has a personality that can be very passionate or out of control. This helps to challenge him and keeps him focused. If he doesn't take things too hard, then he isn't being himself. This attitude should help us to reflect about the way in which we accept ourselves—do we embrace our race, color, economic status, and personality? On the other hand, we can reject traits of our personality that aren't consistent with who we really are. Just as every culture has different customs, each personality has different traits that should be respected and celebrated.

VII. We can focus on, and not hide, our fears when facing big challenges.

During the time when the Big Z was in the minor leagues, there were moments when he didn't want to return to the United States. As told by Julio Figueroa, he missed flights on purpose and felt that he couldn't continue. It wasn't until a game that he pitched against the Texas Rangers and dominated Alex Rodríguez that he declared with serenity and pride, "I belong in this place....If I could dominate Alex [Rodríguez], I can pitch in the major leagues." That evening in the 2002 season was his personal vindication. It's important to state that those feelings were channeled adequately, so we today have a star who is a star because of, not in spite of, his struggles.

When we have the chance to channel our fears adequately, we can better receive encouragement and hope. What would have happened if the Big Z had given up in the middle of his journey? This may happen to baseball players who succumb to their negative feelings or do not have people by them who can motivate them to keep going. We cannot give so much emphasis to the negative ideas that threaten our highest aspirations. We can, with the help of our own self-worth and the power of faith, understand that our fears can work to our benefit. The challenge in front of us is to focus on, label, and target our fears, and, in the right time, let them go.

VIII. We can trust the tools that God gives us.

The Big Z trusts his pitching. He does not underestimate people or regret if he gave the wrong impression at some point. He is going forward, knowing that, like King David, God is in front of him. He celebrates when he does a great job. After boasting about a victory and then losing a game, or just not working hard enough to win the game, he makes fun of it, showing his cheerful side of growing up in Puerto Cabello.

His confidence in his pitching is amazing. It reminds us of David's encounter with Goliath (1 Samuel 17). When the King, just a shepherd, decided to face someone who had threatened God's army, he rejected the weapons that Saul offered him. The shepherd reached for the weapon that he knew well. He was sure that with each stone he threw, he would bring down the giant because he was going against him in the name of the Lord. The Big Z shows that confidence because it is not a superstition, it is a certainty. He knows where his gifts come from and who deserves the glory...and his life gives testimony to that.

CHAPTER 7

NINTH INNING
(FINAL WORDS)

*Not everything is about money....I feel comfortable here...
my family feels good here. This is my town,
my home, my city. I love Chicago. I love the Cubs....
Thank God I can stay here a longer time.*
—The Big Z after signing a multi-year contract

The Hispanic community in the United States has grown rapidly in the last 20 years. According to the 2000 census, Hispanics make up the largest minority in this nation, with 39 million. Chicago is a city with the third-largest Hispanic population, with more than half a million.

Many times, life is hard for Hispanics in the Diaspora, far from their loved ones and the warmth of their land. Many times, life is hostile, and conservative politicians attempt to push legislation that will set barriers and stop minority growth. At the same time, these minorities are providing a strong work force that helps the national economy. There are approximately 11 million illegal immigrants who generate close to $20 million annually for the American economy.

As of today, Carlos has the highest average salary for a pitcher in major league history: he just signed a $91.5 million contract with a vesting option for a sixth year ($18.3 million per year) plus a $5 million signing bonus. He is no longer the underdog of either peers in Venezuela or the United States. Look how far he's come: from not leaving a lasting impression the first time he was seen by the Cubs organization in Puerto Cabello, from being considered a

The Big Z and his agent and friend Tommy Miranda, after the signing of a multi-year contract, in Wrigley Field.

reliever instead of a starting pitcher, to earning more than any other pitcher in the majors.

His preferred option was to stay with the city that opened doors for him in organized baseball. He wants to contribute in getting the World Series title Cubs fans have craved for almost a century.

The Big Z of Venezuela is an example of excellence for his country and for Latin America. Although he is not illegal, and never has been, his life and development, his faith and desire, have given hope to others who, without a talent for sports but with precious gifts from the Lord, can identify with his charisma and development for the good in their lives, their families, and their countries.

Carlos Zambrano has lived a life chosen by God. Without being perfect, he has known where to set his sights and, even with money, he hasn't forgotten where he came from. He has shown the richness of his people to the poverty of the world, proving that it is more important to live for God and His justice rather than for personal interest. The rich in spirit are truly the world's wealthiest.

Dickson Hernández, one of the Big Z's closest friends since childhood, said about him:

I always saw in Carlos, aside from a friend, a leader. When he sets himself to do something, he does it with God's help. He always has God present....When I began to work where I work today, it was very hard. It took a miracle for me to get to work there, and I am very proud of that. I have a family, am stable, and I'm a better person who's been inspired by what Carlos has achieved. He wants to improve Puerto Cabello and will do whatever he can to achieve it....Each time he comes back from Chicago, he finds us and he always knows to be humble, and has never turned his back on us. He knows we would not disappoint him. He wants to communicate God's word to everyone through sports. He says: 'If God has blessed me, I will bless others.'

I finish this story with a personal note to Carlos Zambrano:

Your charisma imposes a great responsibility on you. You have achieved what many people are still struggling to reach: you have a gift and you use it for the edification of the human race. Your achievements in baseball have put a heavy load on you. This load is no different than that of other successful athletes, although they may not be aware of it. The difference between you and the rest is not your gestures on the mound, or that you point to your Savior, it is the deepness of your testimony that sets you apart. It is your spirit that makes you big, beyond your achievements, and far larger than the amount of the big contracts that you will have.

The validity of all this lays on your capability to maintain a sense of justice, love for your people, and respect for those who, like you, did not have a voice. You have the potential of being a voice for those who have not been heard because of inequality, of bringing hope to those who have none. And you can bring to light all those fruits of the Spirit that are working in favor of the rejected, those for whom Jesus died.

There is where you truly are big, Big Z.

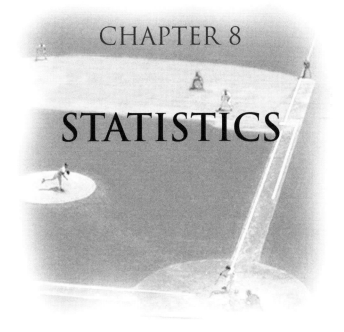

CHAPTER 8

STATISTICS

CARLOS ALBERTO ZAMBRANO

Height:
6'5"

Weight:
255 lbs.

Born:
June 1, 1981

Birthplace:
Puerto Cabello, Estado Carabobo, Venezuela

Bats:
Switch

Throws:
Right

Debut:
August 20, 2001, with the Chicago Cubs

Education:
Escuela Unidad Educative Creación in Puerto Cabello, Venezuela

Christian Upbringing:
Iglesia Evangélica Pentecostal Monte Horeb

MINOR LEAGUE HIGHLIGHTS

MINOR LEAGUE CAREER STATS

Year	Team	ERA	W–L	G	CG	GS	IP	SO
2002	Chicago CubsNL	3.66	4–8	32	0	16	108.1	94
2002	IowaAAA	0	0–0	3	0	0	9	11
2001	Chicago CubsNL	15.26	1–2	6	0	1	7.2	11
2001	IowaAAA	3.87	10–5	26	1	0	151	155
2000	IowaAAA	3.95	2–5	34	0	6	57	46
2000	WestTenn.AA	1.34	3–1	9	0	0	60	43
1999	LansingA	4.18	13–7	27	2	0	153.1	98
1998	AZLCubsR	3.15	0–1	14	0	1	40	36
Total	AAA	3.74	12–10	63	1	6	217	212
	AA	1.34	3–1	9	0	0	60	43
	A	4.18	13–7	27	2	0	153.1	98
	R	3.15	0–1	14	0	1	40	36
Totals	5 seasons	3.52	28–19	113	3	7	470	389

Source: baseball-reference.com

YEAR-BY-YEAR HIGHLIGHTS*

1998

Carlos began his professional career with the Cubs' Mesa (Rookie) club, where he went 0–1 with 1 save and a 3.15

*From www.mlb.com

ERA in 14 games (2 starts). He did not allow any homers in 40.0 innings of work.

1999
Carlos pitched for his first full-season club, going 13–7 with a 4.17 ERA in 27 games for Lansing (A). His team-high victory total tied for second among all Cubs minor league pitchers. He allowed only nine homers in 153.1 innings of work.

2000
• The Big Z reached the Class AAA level at the age of 19, making 34 relief appearances for Iowa (AAA) after opening the campaign in the West Tenn (AA) starting rotation.

• At West Tenn, he went 3–1 with a 1.34 ERA in nine starts, allowing 39 hits in 60.1 innings and holding opponents to a .181 average (39–216).

• He opened the year as the youngest player in Class AA—and was leading the Southern League in ERA when promoted.

• Carlos was utilized solely out of Iowa's bullpen after receiving a May 27 promotion—five days before his 19th birthday—and went 2–5 with six saves and a 3.97 ERA.

• He picked up his first Iowa victory July 1 at Memphis, pitching 3.0 shutout frames in a 7–5 contest. He hit his first professional homer off Dave Wainhouse.

• He worked at least 3.0 innings in four other bullpen outings.

• After the season, he was selected as the seventh-best prospect in the Pacific Coast League by *Baseball America* and also was chosen to the Howe Sportsdata all-prospect and all-teen teams.

2001

• Carlos saw his first major league action, going 1–2 in six games for the Cubs (1 start). He spent most of the campaign in the starting rotation at Iowa (AAA).

• The Cubs' purchased his contract from Iowa on August 20 to start the first game of a double header against Milwaukee. He returned to the majors September 9.

• The Big Z took the loss in his big league debut (10–2), allowing seven runs and four hits in four-plus innings. He didn't allow a hit until the 4th inning.

• Carlos pitched solely out of the bullpen during his second stint with the Cubs. He made his first big league relief appearance September 19 at Cincinnati, working a scoreless frame.

• He picked up his first major league victory in his next outing September 21 at Houston, 12–4.

• In 26 games for Iowa, including 25 starts, he was 10–5 with a 3.88 ERA. His strikeout total (155) ranked third in the Pacific Coast League.

• He allowed just nine homers (1 every 16.7 innings) while holding PCL batters to a .226 average (124–549).

• After his first 11 starts, his ERA stood at 4.38 (31 ER/63.2 IP). Beginning June 14, he allowed 34 earned runs and 64 hits in 87.0 innings for a 3.52 ERA.

• The Big Z fanned 13 batters in a complete-game 3–2 victory at Omaha August 30. He also struck out 13 on May 28 against Salt Lake, allowing three hits in 8.0 innings in a 1–0 victory.

• In an 11–7 victory over Las Vegas on June 8, he hit his second professional home run.

• Carlos earned PCL Pitcher of the Week honors for the week ending August 12 after going 2–0 with a 0.00 ERA in two starts. In victories over Tacoma on August 7 (3–2) and at Nashville on August 11 (2–0), he worked 13.0 innings and allowed nine hits and three walks while striking out 11 batters.

• He was named to the Sporting News' end-of-season Triple-A all-prospect team.

MAJOR LEAGUE HIGHLIGHTS

MAJOR LEAGUE PITCHING STATS

Season	W	L	ERA	G	CG	SHO	IP	H	R	ER	HR	BB	SO
2001	1	2	15.26	6	0	0	7.2	11	13	13	2	8	4
2002	4	8	3.66	32	0	0	108.1	94	53	44	9	63	93
2003	13	11	3.11	32	3	1	214	188	88	74	9	94	168
2004	16	8	2.75	31	1	1	209.2	174	73	64	14	81	188
2005	14	6	3.26	33	2	0	223.1	170	88	81	21	86	202
2006	16	7	3.41	33	0	0	214	162	91	81	20	115	210
2007	15	12	4.26	30	1	0	190.0	167	95	90	21	92	163
Career Totals	79	54	3.45	197	7	2	1167	966	501	447	96	539	1028

MAJOR LEAGUE BATTING STATS

Season	G	AB	R	H	2B	3B	HR	RBI	TB	BB	SO	SB	OBP	SLG	AVG
2001	6	2	0	0	0	0	0	0	0	0	0	0	0	0	0
2002	31	30	0	1	1	0	0	0	2	0	15	0	0.033	0.067	0.033
2003	30	75	9	18	5	0	2	6	29	1	26	0	0.25	0.387	0.24
2004	30	70	8	16	1	0	1	5	20	3	29	0	0.257	0.286	0.229
2005	33	80	8	24	6	2	1	6	37	0	25	0	0.3	0.463	0.3
2006	35	73	9	11	0	0	6	11	29	1	27	1	0.16	0.397	0.151
2007	32	70	8	19	1	0	2	5	26	0	26	0	0.271	0.371	0.271
Career Totals	197	400	42	89	14	2	12	33	143	5	148	1	0.231	0.358	0.223

YEAR-BY-YEAR HIGHLIGHTS

2002

• Carlos spent most of the first half in the Cubs' bullpen, and all of the second half in the starting rotation. In 32 games (16 starts), he went 4–8 with a 3.66 ERA.

• He limited opponents to a .235 average and surrendered nine homers in 108.1 innings.

• The Big Z was 4–8 with a 3.68 ERA in his 16 starts (38 ER/ 93.0 IP).

• He worked at least 6.0 innings in 9 of his starts. In those games, he allowed 12 earned runs and 37 hits in 62.0 innings of work for a 1.74 ERA.

• He worked fewer than 6.0 innings in seven starts. In those contests, he had a 7.55 ERA (26 ER/31.0 IP).

• He saw action in 16 games out of the bullpen, going 0–0 with a 3.52 ERA in 15.1 innings. He retired the first batter he faced in 10 of his appearances and stranded nine of his 13 inherited runners.

• He began the year at Iowa (AAA), but was recalled April 11 to take the place of the injured Kyle Farnsworth. He had pitched in 1 Class AAA contest, working 3.0 scoreless innings on April 7 against New Orleans.

• Carlos joined the starting rotation July 1 at Florida, taking the loss in an 11–1 contest. In the second start of his major league career, he worked 4.2 innings and allowed six hits and six runs (2 earned).

• He earned his first big league win as a starter July 6 at Atlanta (7–3). He allowed two hits over 5.0 scoreless innings while striking out six batters.

• The Big Z defeated the Braves again in his next start July 15 at Wrigley Field (3–2), working 7.0 innings.

• He was a hard-luck loser July 20 against Houston (3–2), working 7.0 innings and allowing three hits, three runs, and one walk while fanning a career-high 10 batters.

• Carlos suffered another tough loss August 9 at Colorado in just the second 2–0 game in Coors Field history. He worked 7.0 innings and allowed just hits, one run, and no walks while striking out two batters. After giving up back-to-back hits to start the bottom of the 1st, he retired 20 of the final 22 batters he faced.

• He was optioned to Iowa August 31 and recalled September 3.

• On September 4 versus Milwaukee, he combined with Antonio Alfonseca in blanking the Brewers 3–0. The win snapped a personal five-game losing streak.

• He worked 8.0 innings and allowed three singles while striking out six. He had a no-hitter for 4.1 innings.

• He recorded his first big league hit in the contest, a double off Nelson Figueroa and opened his career 0-for-22.

• Beginning August 14, the switch-hitter batted solely from the right side of the plate.

• He was on the disabled list May 10 through June 6 with a partial ulnar collateral ligament sprain of his right elbow. He suffered the injury during a May 9 relief appearance against Milwaukee.

2003
• Carlos spent his first full season as a big league starter, going 13–11 with three complete games and a 3.11 ERA. He finished seventh in the National League in ERA and eighth in innings pitched (214.0).

• He finished eighth in the National League in ERA on the road (3.22) and was eighth in home ERA at 3.00. Mark Prior also ranked among the league Top 10 in both categories. Only two Cubs pitchers over the previous 30 seasons finished a season in the National League Top 10 in ERA both at home and on the road: Rick Reuschel (1977) and Greg Maddux (1992).

• Since entering the Cubs' starting rotation just prior to the 2002 All-Star Game, he has posted a 3.28 ERA in 48 starts (112 ER/307.0 IP).

• His wife, Ismari, gave birth to the couple's second child, Catherine, on May 8.

• In 13 starts after the All-Star break, he was 7–3 with three complete games and a 2.51 ERA (26 ER/93.1 IP). In 93.1 innings of work, he allowed five homers.

• He won five consecutive starts July 20 through August 12. It was the first winning streak of more than two games during his big league career.

• In his first two starts of the second half, he allowed one earned run in 14.2 innings and was 4-for-7 at the plate with a homer and 4 RBI.

• In the Cubs' 16–2 victory at Florida July 20, he allowed one run in 6.1 innings and went 3-for-4 with a double and 2 RBI. As part of his first career multi-hit contest, he had two hits in the Cubs' six-run 3rd inning. He began the frame with a double off Dontrelle Willis, then drove in the final run of the inning with a single off Tommy Phelps.

• In a 5–3 victory at Houston on July 25, he worked 8.1 innings and allowed five hits, three 1st-inning unearned runs and one walk while striking out seven batters. He retired 24 of the final 26 batters he faced and tied the game at 3–3 with a 7th-inning two-run homer off Wade Miller. The homer came on an 0–2 pitch.

• The Big Z hurled the first complete game and shutout of his major league career in a 3–0 victory over Houston on August 12. In his 9.0 innings of work, he allowed five hits and two walks while striking out 10 batters, which tied his career high.

• In a 4–1 win on August 22 at Arizona, he flirted with a no-hitter, throwing just 93 pitches in his second route-going effort. In his 9.0 innings of work, he allowed three hits, one run, and two walks while fanning four batters.

• He started the Cubs' first-ever contest at San Juan's Hiram Bithorn Stadium on September 9, working 7.0 innings in defeating Montreal 4–3.

• Carlos allowed just nine homers in 214.0 innings of work— an average of one run surrendered every 23.8 innings.

• The only other full-season big league starter with fewer than 10 homers allowed was Boston's Pedro Martinez (seven in 186.2 innings).

• Since 1950, the only Cubs starter to work more than 200.0 innings and allow fewer than 10 homers was Greg Maddux in 1992 (seven homers in 268.0 innings).

• He gave up six runs against St. Louis on May 9 (7.1-inning stint), five runs in 6.0 innings on June 6 against the Yankees, five runs in a 6.0-inning outing on July 3 at Philadelphia, seven runs in five-plus innings on July 13 versus Atlanta, and nine runs (six earned) in 4.2 innings on September 19 at Pittsburgh.

• His ERA in his other 27 starts was 2.19 (45 ER/185.0 IP).

• He homered twice in 2003—once batting right-handed (on May 3 off Colorado's Darren Oliver) and once batting left-handed (on July 25 off Houston's Wade Miller). He was the first switch-hitting pitcher in club annals to homer from both sides of the plate in one season.

• At 21 years of age on Opening Day, Zambrano was the youngest Cub to appear on the Cubs' season-opening roster since Greg Maddux (20) in 1987.

• On May 3 against Colorado (in which he had a no-decision in a 6–4 Cubs loss), he hit his first major league homer—and the third of his professional career—when he connected for a 4th-inning solo shot off Darren Oliver.

• He picked up his fifth win of the season on May 25 at Houston (7–3). He was the winning pitcher just four times the year before.

• On June 22 against the White Sox, he allowed one run in 8.0 innings in a 2–1 win.

2004

• The Big Z, who was honored with his first career All-Star selection in just his third full season in the majors, won a career-high 16 games and posted a career-best 2.75 ERA.

• He finished fourth in the National League in ERA and tied for fifth in wins. He also was sixth in opponents batting average against (.225), eighth in strikeouts (188) and strikeouts per 9.0 innings (8.1), ninth in hit batsmen (20), and tied for ninth in walks (81).

• He was third in the National League in ERA in home games (2.38), sixth in road ERA (3.13), and second in day ERA (2.01).

• Carlos surpassed the 200.0-innings mark for the second straight season, as he hurled 214.0 innings in 2003 and 209.2 innings in 2004.

• He held right-handed opponents to a .218 average and had a .198 average in home games.

• He was 10–2 in 15 games at Wrigley Field, lowering his career ERA at the Friendly Confines to 3.30.

• He was selected National League Pitcher of the Month in September.

• He went 4–0 with a 1.01 ERA (4 ER/35.2 IP) in five starts.

• He struck out 28 batters while issuing 11 walks—and held opponents to a .211 average.

• Carlos went 9–4 with a 2.61 ERA in the first half of the season en route to being named to his first All-Star team.

• At 23 years and 43 days old, Zambrano was the youngest Cub to ever appear in an All-Star Game.

• He worked the 4th inning of the Midsummer Classic, surrendering an RBI-triple to Alex Rodriguez.

• The Big Z worked 6.0 or more innings in 26 of his 31 starts, including his second career complete-game shutout.

• He hurled a two-hitter May 7 against Colorado (11–0). Matt Holliday singled in the 5th inning for the Rockies' first hit. Aaron Miles had the only other hit for Colorado (in the 9th). Carlos struck out five batters and did not issue a walk in the contest.

• He made his first start of the 2004 campaign April 9 at Atlanta, allowing just one run in 7.0 innings. He was not involved in the decision, despite giving up just 2 hits and striking out 7 batters. The Cubs won the 2–1 contest in the 15th inning on Todd Hollandsworth solo pinch-homer.

• He beat Pittsburgh for the first time in six career starts on April 15, holding the Pirates to one run and one walk in earning his first win of the season (10–5).

• He struck out a career-high 12 batters May 2 at St. Louis for his fourth career double-digit strikeout game. He was not involved in the decision in a 1–0 loss, though he hurled 7.0 shutout innings and allowed just three hits and three walks.

• Carlos battled dehydration in pitching the Cubs to a 6–2 victory over the crosstown rival White Sox.

• For the second time in his career, he flirted with a no-hitter, on August 23, against Milwaukee. Geoff Jenkins' 7th-inning, one-out double was the first hit he gave up. He went on to allow three runs on four hits and struck out nine in the 8–3 final.

• He hit his third career home run September 17 in Cincinnati off Mike Matthews in the 12–4 Cubs win. And he allowed just one run in his 7.0 innings of work.

2005

• The Big Z struck out 200 for the first time in his career. One of his best games was one in which he didn't get a decision. On July 22, he and St. Louis's Chris Carpenter both went nine innings. The Big Z matched his career high with 12 strikeouts, and both starters gave up one run each. The Cubs won in extra innings. He went 8–2 with a 2.65 ERA in the second half.

2006

• Carlos matched his career high with 16 wins, despite going winless in his first six starts in April.

• He was 6–0 with a 4.15 ERA in July and won Pitcher of the Month honors. He ranked among the National League leaders in ERA, strikeouts, and wins, but also was first in walks. Zambrano did better away from Wrigley Field, posting a 9–1 road record and a 2.97 ERA.

Since entering the Cubs' starting rotation just prior to the 2002 All-Star Game, Carlos has posted a 3.07 ERA in 79 starts (176 ER/516.2 IP), with an average of more than 6.5 innings per outing. He was selected to the National League All-Star for the first time in 2004. He was the youngest Cub in franchise history to pitch in an All-Star Game. He was honored as the National League Pitcher of the Month for September 2004. When he made his Cubs/major league debut as a 20-year-old on August 20, 2001, he became the first player born during the decade of the 1980s to appear in a game for the Cubs.

FIRST FIVE YEARS IN THE MAJORS

Player	W	L	G	ERA
Carlos Zambrano	**48**	**35**	**134**	**3.26**
Roger Clemens	78	34	140	3.19
Wilson Álvarez	35	22	100	3.78
Randy Johnson	49	48	159	4.24
Steve Carlton	47	34	119	2.75
Freddie García	72	45	155	3.98
Johan Santana	43	18	151	3.98
Kerry Wood (2001–2005)	49	41	142	3.63
Mark Prior (2002–2005)	41	23	97	3.36
Josh Beckett	41	34	106	3.46
Pedro Martínez	48	31	154	3.09